The Financial Times Guide to Analysis for Managers

The Financial Times Guide to Analysis for Managers

Effective planning tools and techniques

Babette E. Bensoussan
and Craig S. Fleisher

**Financial Times
Prentice Hall
is an imprint of**

Harlow, England • London • New York • Boston • San Francisco • Toronto • Sydney • Singapore • Hong Kong
Tokyo • Seoul • Taipei • New Delhi • Cape Town • Madrid • Mexico City • Amsterdam • Munich • Paris • Milan

Pearson Education Limited

Edinburgh Gate
Harlow
Essex CM20 2JE
England

and Associated Companies throughout the world

Visit us on the World Wide Web at:
www.pearsoned.co.uk

Original edition, entitled ANALYSIS WITHOUT PARALYSIS: 10 TOOLS TO MAKE BETTER STRATEGIC DECISIONS, 1st Edition, by BENSOUSSAN, BABETTE E.; FLEISHER, CRAIG S., published by Pearson Education, Inc. publishing as FT Press, Copyright © 2008.

This edition published by PEARSON EDUCATION LTD, Copyright © 2009.

This edition is manufactured in Great Britain and is authorised for sale only in UK, Europe, Middle East and Africa.

The rights of Babette Bensoussan and Craig Fleisher to be identified as authors of this work have been asserted by them in accordance with the Copyright, Designs and Patents Act 1988.

ISBN: 978-0-273-72201-4

British Library Cataloguing-in-Publication Data
A catalogue record for this book is available from the British Library

10 9 8 7 6 5 4 3 2 1
13 12 11 10 09

Typeset in Stone Serif by 3
Printed by Ashford Colour Press Ltd, Gosport

The publisher's policy is to use paper manufactured from sustainable forests.

This book is dedicated to our families

Contents

The authors / ix
Acknowledgements / xi

PART I INTRODUCTION / 1

1 Business management and the role of analysis / 3

2 The analysis process / 13

Part II ANALYSIS TOOLS / 21

3 BCG growth/share portfolio matrix / 23

4 Competitor analysis / 39

5 Driving forces analysis / 53

6 Financial ratio and statement analysis / 67

7 Five Forces Industry Analysis / 89

8 Issue analysis / 101

9 Product life cycle analysis / 117

10 Scenario analysis / 135

11 Macroenvironmental (STEEP/PEST) analysis / 149

12 **SWOT analysis** / 159

13 **Value chain analysis** / 171

14 **Win/loss analysis** / 189

Index / 201

The authors

Babette E. Bensoussan is Managing Director of The MindShifts Group, a company specialising in competitive intelligence, strategic planning and strategic marketing projects in the Australasia region. Babette is widely recognised and sought after for her international expertise in competitive analysis and has provided mentoring and training to executives and organisations to assist with the delivery and implementation of competitive intelligence. She has undertaken major studies for and consulted to Australian and global Fortune 500 companies and has undertaken over 300 projects in a wide range of industries and markets.

In 2006 she was recognised for her work in this field by being presented with the highest and most prestigious award in the field of competitive intelligence – the SCIP Meritorious Award.

Apart from her active business responsibilities, Babette has taught competitive intelligence at both the Sydney Graduate School of Management, University of Western Sydney, and at Bond University in the undergraduate business and MBA programmes. She has published numerous articles on strategic planning, competitive intelligence and strategic marketing, and is an invited speaker and guest lecturer both domestically and internationally.

Babette has shared her knowledge of competitive business analysis by co-authoring two books. *Strategic and Competitive Analysis* and *Business and Competitive Analysis* have both been the top-selling books in this field since being published in 2003 and 2007 respectively.

Craig S. Fleisher holds the Windsor Research Leadership Chair and is Professor of Management at the Odette School of Business, University of Windsor, Canada. Recognised as one of Canada's top MBA professors by Canadian Business, he has variously served as dean, MBA director and endowed research chair at several Canadian universities, is a docent of the Institute of Business Information Management and Logistics at Tampere University of Technology in Finland, and held or holds adjunct positions at universities in Australia, New Zealand, South Africa and the United Kingdom. His PhD is from the Katz Graduate School of Business, University of Pittsburgh. A contributing member of various association, corporate and journal editorial boards, he is a past President and Fellow of the international Society of Competitive Intelligence Professionals, founder and inaugural chair of the Board of Trustees of the Competitive Intelligence Foundation (Washington, DC), founding editor of the *Journal of Competitive Intelligence and Management*, and founding member of the International Association of Business and Society. Recognised as the 2007 Advisor of the Year in Canada by the Golden Key International Honour Society, Craig has authored or edited nine books (several also have multiple foreign language translations) and scores of articles and chapters in the area of applied strategy, competitive intelligence and analysis, or performance management. His most recent book was *Business and Competitive Analysis* (FT Press, 2007). A well-travelled speaker, he regularly advises leading corporations, associations and public sector agencies on competitive intelligence and analysis.

Acknowledgements

To write this book I have had to stand on the shoulders of many – my co-author Craig Fleisher who gave me so much support and understanding during my moments of crisis; my wonderful husband whose patience, nurturing and understanding provided a safe space for me to work; my family and dear friends who understood the many times I was not always there for them while completing this book. To the many shoulders at FT Press, thank you for making this book happen. We could not have done it without you. And, finally, I would like to thank my many clients and colleagues for the challenges and questioning that made me realise there had to be a simpler way to do business analysis without being left in a state of paralysis. I hope this little book provides you with the necessary tools to solve some of your problems.

Babette Bensoussan

I would like to thank my long-time co-author and friend Babette Bensoussan for all her hard and thoughtful work toward making this book a reality. She worked tirelessly while also balancing numerous other assignments, issues and tasks. I also want to thank my family members, friends and colleagues for remaining patient and understanding during the time that I was working on completing the book. Members of FT Press have also been their usual helpful selves throughout the duration of this writing effort. I also want to thank individuals at several universities who have been working with and supportive of me, mainly including the Leicester Business School – De Montfort University (UK) and my good friend Sheila Wright, with whom I am sharing in the supervision of several doctoral students as well as numerous research projects; and Tampere University of Technology (Finland) and Mika Hannula, who directs the of the Institute of Business Information Management and Logistics, where I am appointed as a docent and also participate in the annual eBRF conferences. Last, but not least, I want to express my appreciation to the various bodies that provided funding and other forms of support to me along the way in developing this book, especially the University of Windsor through its Windsor Research Leadership Chair and Odette Research Chairs and Dean Allan Conway in the Odette School of Business, who has been generous in allowing me to pursue the completion of this book.

Craig S. Fleisher

Many of the techniques included in this book were conceptualised by leading economists, financial and cost accountants, futurists, business professors, consultants, and other insightful practitioners or theoreticians. They often developed their ideas in an effort to solve pressing analytical problems that they faced. We are grateful to these individuals for enlightening our understanding of strategic and competitive analysis and make a sincere attempt to acknowledge the originators of these techniques in the book. Nevertheless, there are times when accurately making this acknowledgement can be difficult, such as when the technique (for example, SWOT) was quickly and widely accepted and came to form the commonly held body of knowledge underlying organisational decision making.

Introduction

1

Business management and the role of analysis

In today's information age, businessmen and businesswomen must increasingly be able to make sense of their competition, environments, organisations and strategies in order to be successful. Business management is a way of conducting an organisation that has as an ultimate objective the development of values, managerial capabilities, organisational responsibilities and administrative systems that link strategic, tactical and operational decision making at all hierarchical levels and across all lines of authority.

One of the key tasks of today's business executives is to participate in and contribute to their organisations' strategies. Sadly, strategy is an overused word that means different things to different people. Even distinguished management scholars and senior executives can be hard pressed to define it or agree on what it entails.

Although we really do not want to muddy the waters and add further to the lengthy list of definitions out there, we do know with confidence that winning strategies are based on originality and uniqueness – being 'different' to competitors in ways that customers value. The idea of these differences has been defined by economists to mean competencies and, in strategic management terms, this means trying to develop distinctive organisational resources and competencies. These competencies should then be leveraged through clearly thought-out strategies into a competitive advantage in light of the organisation's market.

A competitive advantage is the distinct way an organisation is positioned in the market to obtain an edge over its competitors. This status is most commonly evidenced by the organisation's ability to generate and maintain sustained levels of profitability above the industry average. The process that is primarily associated with helping an organisation to attain competitive advantage is strategic planning, which can be defined as a disciplined and systematic effort to fulfil specifications of an organisation's strategy as well as the assignment of responsibilities for its execution. This process is shown in Figure 1.1.

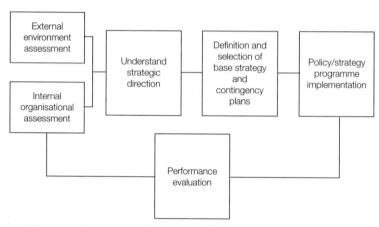

Figure 1.1 A generic strategic planning process

Management decisions in the strategy development process are concerned with the following:

■ *The scope of the organisation's activities.* Where are we going to operate? What customers will we target? Which competitors will we avoid? What parts of the value chain will we emphasise? What will we do ourselves and what will we outsource?

■ *The matching of an organisation's activities to its environment.* This is the idea of finding a strategy that creates a desirable level of 'fit'.

■ *The matching of an organisation's activities to its resource capability.* This requires working within our means while winning customers and generating profits.

■ *The implications for change throughout the organisation.* These are likely to be complex in nature and will require excellence in execution or strategy implementation.

■ *The allocation and reallocation of significant resources of an organisation.* This requires us to seek resource optimisation in using our assets where they can be maximised.

■ *The values, expectations and goals of those influencing strategy.* This means that decision makers understand what is happening and have a clear sense of where the organisation needs to go both now and into the future.

■ *The direction the organisation will move in the long run.* This can be over five to ten years or more, depending on the nature of change and competition affecting an industry.

Within this process, management decisions may differ depending on the timing and the responsibility of the decision makers. These decisions would most commonly be identified as strategic, tactical or operational. By this we mean:

■ **Strategic decisions** have significant resource allocation impact, set precedents or the tone for decisions further down the organisation, are infrequent in nature and may actually be irreversible, and have a potentially material effect on the organisation's competitiveness within its marketplace. They are made by top managers and affect the business direction of the organisation.

■ **Tactical decisions** are less all-encompassing than strategic ones and involve formulating and implementing policies for the organisation. They are usually made by mid-level managers and often materially affect functions such as marketing, accounting, production, or a business unit or product as opposed to the entire organisation. Tactical decisions generally have lesser resource implications than strategic decisions.

■ **Operational decisions** support the day-to-day decisions needed to operate the operational organisation and take effect over a few days or weeks. Typically made by a lower-level manager, operational decisions are distinct from tactical and strategic decisions in that they are made frequently and often 'on the fly'. Operational decisions tend to be highly structured, often with well-defined procedure manuals or within readily understood parameters.

Finding the means for achieving this 'fit' or congruence between an organisation and its (business or competitive) environment is a critical task of any senior executive and requires sound analytical efforts and some thinking about the global environment in which the organisation competes.

No senior executive can be expected to know the entire competitive terrain well enough to correctly call all the shots. Within today's complex, chaotic, globally competitive environment, the pressing need for making sense, strategic thinking and improved understanding of the competitive terrain is why organisations need to develop and enhance their analytical abilities.

Analysis needs to be done well to help organisations succeed.

But isn't analysis something that everyone learns during schooling or on the job? Can't we just get by like everybody else and rely solely on our intuition, gut, experience and so on to succeed well into the future?

The answer to these questions is 'No' – and particularly not these days. See Table 1.1 for a brief explaination of what we do and do not mean by analysis.

As a minimum, good analysis of your competition, environment, organisation and strategy should help you deliver the following:

- early warning of potentially developing opportunities or emerging threats in your competitive environment
- an objective and arm's-length assessment of your organisation's relative competitive position
- the ability to help your organisation adapt more quickly and easily to changes in the environment
- the means for basing your organisation's strategic, marketing, sales or product plans on relevant and timely insights
- confidence that decisions are based on systematically derived understanding that reduces ambiguity and complexity to low levels.

The driving purpose of performing analysis is to better understand your industry, context and competitors in order to make better decisions. Improving the quality of decision making should hopefully improve the quality of strategies that provide a competitive advantage, which in turn delivers performance results that are superior to your competitors'.

The output of any analysis should be actionable – that is, future-oriented – and should help decision makers to develop better competitive strategies and tactics. Analysis results should also facilitate a better understanding than competitors have of the competitive environment, and identify current and future competitors, specifically their plans and strategies. *The ultimate aim of analysis is to produce better business results!*

Table 1.1 Identifying analysis

	*What analysis **is***	*What analysis is **not***
Methods	The practiced aplication of proven technologies.	Constant usage of industry conventions and one-off solutions.
Process	A method and set of steps designed to effectively break a situation into its component elements and recompose it in a way that addresses a challenge or question.	'We just kind of know what it is, how to do it and, fortunately, have managed to get by so far.' 'We hire consultants to do it for us.'
Output	Actionable insight, intelligence/ meaning and implications derived from data and information.	Repackaged, reorganised, reclassified data and information. Often a summary of the information at hand. No meaningful conversion.
Data sources	Legal and ethical gathering of relevant data or information driven by the needs defined in the structuring of the analytical question.	Seeking and using data or information from illegal sources or by unethical means – often incomplete.
Support systems	Using application-relevant communication, information and management systems to supplement your thinking.	A software application or solution you can aquire and apply 'off the shelf'. Magic-bullet solutions.
Timing	Provided in advance of any decisions.	Rushed to provide support to an answer that has been decided.
Communica-tion channel	Conducted in whatever means the decision maker can best accept and use it.	Done via 'formal' reports with a specific format. Always in writing.
Questions answered	What? So what? Now what?	Just something nice to know – providing no insights.
Catalyst	Yours or your boss' discussed need to know something. The need to better position your organisation in its competitive marketplace.	What you think or hope is important to the executive. The need to demonstrate we are actually doing something.

The increasing need for effective analysis

As indicated earlier, getting business results from analysis has become a more important facet of competitiveness in recent years due to a number of important reasons.

First, globalisation has increased the absolute level of competition present in most marketplaces. In the past, a competitor could sustain marketplace advantages by being in the right place at the right time. Geographic, physical and sociopolitical barriers kept competitors at bay and out of many marketplaces. Most of these barriers are falling or have fallen in light of the vast progress made in communication, information systems, trade policy and transport. New competitors quickly appear when and where these marketplace barriers fade.

And new competitors may compete very differently from existing competitors. They may have learned their business in different contexts, often faced different customer demands, utilised unique resources, and understood competition based on these unique contexts and experiences. No longer can organisations expect competitors to compete by age-old 'rules of the game' or the 'same old' industry means of competing. Sometimes, the form of competition may not even appear logical, insightful or ethical, yet all the while being legal. Because of this new global competition, the need to thoroughly understand competitors and business contexts grows in importance.

Second, the global economy is increasingly being characterised as a *knowledge economy*. A paradigm shift, whereby a large proportion of individuals have changed their way of seeing the world and see it now from a new shared perspective, has occurred as we move further away from the industrial economy paradigm that dominated most of the last two centuries. As opposed to producing tangible 'things' with plants, property and equipment, services and related 'intangibles' associated with people and what they know now constitute the largest part of GDP in most of the leading economies, and services are more knowledge based than material based.

Many companies are amassing data and information while at the same time not recognising that *knowledge* is not the same thing as *information*. Because of improvements in communication channels, information is available in previously unseen quantities. Information has become increasingly infused with noise, redundancy and ambiguity, and is of lower value. It is a product in what economists call a 'state of oversupply' in most developed economies, and this is also becoming true in lesser developed economies. Sustaining a competitive advantage requires companies to uniquely apply data and information, to create order out of chaos and complexity, and to leverage and transfer knowledge while striving toward acquiring expertise.

Knowledge is the capacity to act. The conversion of knowledge to business insights and action requires competence in analysis or sense making. Competence embraces such things as experience, factual understanding about industry and organisational conditions, decision-making and managerial skills, and making insightful value judgements. Competence is developed through making mistakes, practice, reflection, repetition and training. More than ever before, the knowledge economy means that organisations will need to develop further their resources, abilities, competence and, ultimately, expertise if they intend to gain or sustain a competitive advantage.

Third, the new economy is characterised by increasing imitability, whereby competitors have a greater ability than ever before to quickly replicate and copy most facets of a new product or service offering. Fending off imitators is increasingly difficult because of market complexity and the subsequent need to involve other organisations in alliances, collaborations with competitors, spin-offs, and ever-changing outsourcing and staffing arrangements between organisations. As a result of the protection of a product or service through legally recognised vehicles such as copyrights, patents and trademarks, it is now easy for a competitor to manufacture around a new offering because so much information about its inner workings is available publicly. Finding this information has also become easier in an age where governments and international agencies must share this information with one another to establish the legal viability of a new offering. More than a few companies succeed by being 'quick seconds' or 'fast followers' into the marketplace and stressing their competitive abilities at quickly offering an improved product or service after the originator.

Fourth, there are the problems and opportunities caused by increasing complexity and speed. Underlying the changing marketplace is communication and information technology that allows the transfer of data to take place at faster rates than ever before. But while this change in mechanical means has happened, the human ability to process data has remained essentially stable.

A decade or two ago a company could establish a formidable lead for several years by introducing new products or services. Today, a company's time at the top in a market-leading position has shrunk to a much shorter duration; in other words, the interval a company enjoys as 'market leader' has fallen to previously unforeseen levels. The cycle time underlying the introduction of new products or services is also shorter, and companies have to continue reducing it while at the same time increasing the number of introductions they make to stay ahead of competitors.

Concluding observations

As we stated earlier, all of these factors necessitate good competitive insights. And good competitive insights require effective analysis. Successful business analysis requires understanding environments, industries and organisations. This comes from, among other things, experience, solid data and information, and the proper choice and utilisation of analytical techniques.

Today's businesspeople need to do a better job of making sure that the analysis they perform is based on sound, proven methodologies. Hopefully in the future you will master a core set of methodologies that will make the way you evaluate data and information more effective and more decision relevant. At a minimum, after reading this book, you will know at least 12 methodologies to help you on your path.

This book contains 12 of the more well-known and heavily utilised analytical techniques for assessing the external and internal organisational environments (see Figure 1.1) and is designed to assist any businessperson who needs to develop insights and make sense of the business environment. It is based on our many decades of experience consulting, practising and researching how business and competitive analysis is used in all types of enterprises, whether public or private, or large, medium or small.

Our underlying premise throughout this book is that businesspeople working in any environment must have a robust and healthy selection of tools and techniques to help them answer important questions about their enterprises' abilities to compete, not only in the present but also in the future.

Uniquely, this book focuses specifically on analysis. It is not designed to be another business management or strategic planning text; at the same time we must admit that the processes and techniques described herein can certainly benefit strategic planners and managers. There are plenty of good titles on these topics available in most bookstores, and we routinely refer to many of them ourselves. What surprises us, though, about competitive and strategic analysis, is the limited number of tools and techniques used by most businesspeople and how little genuine insight results from them, when they have scores of techniques at their disposal!

These adverse results occur not only because some tools are badly chosen, outdated or incorrectly used but also because they are misunderstood or misapplied. Even those individuals who get a good business school education may not have had the appropriate contexts, instruction, experiences or guidance in employing these techniques effectively to deal with 'real-world' sense-making challenges.

This book provides instruction on a range of tools and techniques, evaluation of each technique's strengths and weaknesses, as well as an outline of the process used to actually employ the technique. It also includes sample applications, resulting overall in that vital ingredient – insight.

Being a businessperson in an enterprise facing a high degree of competitive rivalry is difficult, especially if an individual is inexperienced or lacks appreciation of the art of analysis. And the analytical challenge for businesspeople today is more daunting than ever for a number of reasons, including the following:

■ *Pressure for a quick judgement.* Competitors are moving fast, investors and shareholders want the quarterly performance targets on time, customers want solutions yesterday – and nobody is willing to wait. Time is the most precious resource for businesspeople; consequently, time will always be in short supply. Decisions are often made on the basis of 'what we know now' because the situation simply does not allow for delay. As such, you need to constantly seek established data collection and classification systems that can provide reliable outputs quickly. Businesspeople everywhere need to address the increasingly time-starved context within which they work and assess its ramifications.

■ *Highly ambiguous situations.* Ambiguity comes in many forms. It can emanate from the nature of competition, the range of competitive tactics employed, key stakeholders' responses in a competitive arena, product or process enhancements, consumer responses to competitive tactics and so on. These types of interjections have been studied by researchers, who have recognised that ambiguity can be a potent barrier to competitive imitation and allow a competitor to sustain an advantage for a longer period.

■ *Incrementally received/processed information.* Rarely will you get the information you need in time and in the format you require. The inability of traditional executive information systems to capture, classify and rank rumours, gossip, grapevine data and knowledge held by employees means that you may lack the kind of primary source information that has always been the 'jewel in the crown' element that makes analysis so valuable.

Excellent analysis is the key to successful business insights and good insights can provide high-value, anticipatory decision support capability in contemporary enterprises. Insight about customers, competitors, potential partners, suppliers and other influential stakeholders is a company's first – and often only – line of attack or defence. Maintaining this capability into the future requires business executives to exploit every opportunity to deliver analysis that is persuasive, relevant, timely, perceptive and action-able.

Analytical outputs must provide the decision-making process with the essential insight needed to preserve an organisation's competitiveness and highlight early warning signs of market changes. We expect that this book will provide you with some helpful guidance and assistance in delivering improved insights to support your organisation's competitive endeavours and in achieving market sense-making objectives.

2

The analysis process

Analysis is the ugly duckling of effective management. Few management authors write about analysis, not many people want to talk about it, and even fewer people claim to be expert at it. Just compare the commercial availability and visibility of data analysis to data collection. Data collectors are found on every street corner, data collection methods are common and available to most takers, and data collection agencies are plentiful. Don't believe us? Go to your local library, search the Internet or read the commercial adverts in your industry magazines.

Why then has analysis got a poor reputation? We think there is a number of reasons that can potentially explain why analysis is not among the most popular topics of discussion at the executive dinner table. In addition to the reasons we identified in Chapter 1, these include the following:

- *Analysis is hard to do for most people.* As in nature, people tend to prefer taking the path of least resistance when it comes to putting forth effort or expending energy. In today's turbo-charged digital world, it is far easier to collect a lot of data than it is to work out what to do with them. This helps explain why one of the fastest growing industries globally during the past decade has been digital storage.

- *Few people have publicly recognised or established analysis expertise.* Even those who do may not necessarily be able to 'teach' or disseminate how to do it. Analysis skills can be developed over time as one grows in experience and knowledge.

- *There are few frameworks for understanding how the analysis component can be managed as an integral part of the decision-making process.* Few individuals can thoughtfully explain how analysis can be successfully managed according to the 'three E's' – efficiency, effectiveness and efficacy. It's a bit like riding a bicycle: many people just jump on and ride, but they cannot explain how they do it to the novice or the four-year-old child hoping to get rid of her training wheels.

It is our view and the findings of several large-scale business surveys that data collection is managed far more successfully than analysis. We see a number of prevalent symptoms that suggest why analysis is not managed properly:

- *Tool rut*. Like the person who has a hammer and begins to think everything he sees looks like a nail, people keep using the same tools over and over again. We describe this tendency to overuse the same tools as being in the 'tool rut'. This is counter to the principle that, in addressing the complexity of this ever-changing world, businesspeople need to look at numerous models to provide value.

- *B-school recipe*. Many individuals charged with doing analysis come out of MBA programmes where they have been offered tried-and-tested recipes from instructors with financial and management accounting backgrounds. Strategy and competitive analysis are as different from accounting analysis as strategy is from accounting.

- *Ratio blinders*. Most businesspeople do analysis based on historical data and financial ratios. This can at best only provide comparison and tell them the size of the gap (the '*what*') between two organisations on a particular data point or data set. It does not help explain the reasons for why the gap exists or how to close it.

- *Convenience shopping*. Individuals frequently do analysis on the basis of the data they have as opposed to the data they *should* have. Because they have certain data at their disposal, they use the analytical technique that suits the data rather than focus the analysis on their questions or the insights actually required. This is especially true when accountants are asked to do analysis and they provide outputs that only reflect financial manipulations.

As mentioned in Chapter 1, this is a book about analysis, and we do know that using this term often makes most businesspeople we advise and teach uncomfortable, particularly when we get past the smoke-and-mirrors level at which most people talk.

With the pace of change in today's global competitive environment, organisations are constantly repositioning themselves so as to stay ahead of or to catch up with their competition. As a result, organisations have a need to better understand and make sense of their environments and of their own evolving and dynamic positions within them. This is the primary objective underlying the process of analysis.

Analysis is without a doubt one of the more difficult and critical roles a manager is called upon to perform. Although, as mentioned here, great strides have been made in recent years in terms of planning projects and collecting data, the same cannot be said for analysis.

As with the type of research formally taught to scientists, the analysis process can be viewed as holding much in common with the scientific method. Analysts observe certain events, persons or actions; develop a proposition or hypothesis to explain what they have observed; and then use the hypothesis to make predictions about what may subsequently occur. These predictions can then be further assessed through additional observations or data, and the hypotheses can be modified based on the results.

As identified earlier, business management involves all aspects of a business. It requires a knowledge and understanding of the environmental impacts on an organisation to ensure that correct decisions are made and taken. It is not only just about looking at best fit but also of taking into account the needs of different stakeholders and diagnosing factors required to create a good outcome.

So how do you formulate strategies and ensure they are the right ones? It is only through the careful collection, examination and evaluation of the facts that appropriate alternatives can be weighed in light of organisational resources and requirements.

In today's world of information overload, collection of data or information is not, in the authors' opinion, the key issue. Instead, it is the examination and evaluation of the information through analysis that is the key to defining appropriate strategies and decisions. This process requires skill, time and effort. While most organisations gather some forms of competitive information, surprisingly few formally analyse it and integrate the results into their ongoing business decision-making and strategy development processes.

What is analysis?

When we use the word analysis, we mean the separation of the whole into its constituent parts to understand each part's value, kind, quantity or quality. It is not just about reasoning from the universal or general to the particular; nor is it about summarising the information collected. It is about breaking down an issue into its parts. Today's executive mindset says that every organisation needs to have at least some professionals who are actively engaged in evaluating and examining each part.

How does one engage in evaluating and examining each part?

Analysis is a multifaceted, multidisciplinary combination of scientific and nonscientific processes by which an individual interprets the data or information to provide meaningful insights. It is used to derive correlations, evaluate trends and patterns, identify performance gaps, and above all to identify and evaluate opportunities available to organisations. Analysis answers that critical 'so what?' question about the data we gather and brings insight to bear directly on the decision-making process.

Effective analysis requires experience, good inputs, intuition, models and, some would argue, even a dash of good luck. It requires constantly varying combinations of art and science, common sense and informed models, and intuition and instruction.

The reason we do analysis is that, although there may be plenty of information around, the issues being analysed are often quite complex, and the overall reality of the situation may not be all that obvious at first glance.

Figure 2.1 identifies a generic approach to analysis.

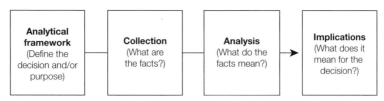

Figure 2.1 A generic approach to analysis

As a process, analysis depends upon raw data. However, using just any data will not lead to effective analysis. The data collected and used to respond to your requirements need to be assessed for its accuracy and reliability.

You need to be aware that understanding accuracy means recognising that not all data are of equal quality. Some data may be excellent, some marginal, some may be bad, and some might even be intended to deceive. Your data sources must be assessed to know whether input data are accurate and reliable.

Sources often have different reasons for supplying data. Knowing the reason that lies under an individual or group's data is important in establishing the fit of these purposes for analysis. Some data sources can be notorious for projecting biases on to data sets. For example, advocacy groups that have policy agendas are often prejudiced in the data they provide to policy makers, sometimes leaving out data that counter their positions while over-emphasising data in support of their positions. As you can appreciate, effective analysis relies on effective data collection.

Apart from good data collection, there is no 'one best way' to perform analysis. We have met our share of individuals who have wanted to drink from the mythical 'analysis spring'. The mythical spring, more popularly known as software, that will reliably do the analysis task, does not exist, and we strongly doubt that it ever will. Despite this, we do believe it is possible to improve your expertise in this process by attending to such things as:

- how to select and sort data and informational inputs (that is, the 'need to know' from the 'nice to know' or 'who cares about knowing' items)
- what analytical technique to apply to a particular need
- what must be understood in effectively informing organisational decisions.

Good analysis simply comes from ongoing practise. The more you practise the techniques in this book, the better you will be able to undertake each technique, and the better will be the quality of your insights.

Whether the application of the analytical techniques can achieve its potential usefulness depends on a number of factors. Based on our experience and understanding of the application of these techniques, there are several warnings to be heeded in performing formal analysis.

First, many organisations have utilised formal methods as a means of taking 'superficial shortcuts' to management decision making. The methods we describe in this book are all based on empirical research and are supported by solid theory developed across a range of managerial disciplines. By presenting the methods individually and in a simplified fashion as we have in this book, we do not mean to suggest that their application can lead to 'magic bullet' answers.

Second, there is no one right analytical tool for every situation. The depth and complexity of analysis is dependent upon the business situation and your needs. It is important that you understand your needs clearly first. No method by itself will provide all the answers needed by executives intent on improving their competitiveness. Analytical techniques nearly always have to be used for specific purposes and in various combinations to obtain optimal results.

Third, you should be wary of becoming overly reliant on a small number of techniques. This is especially prevalent with inexperienced analysts and can happen for a few main reasons, including:

■ generating positive results from the application of a particular technique

■ developing a level of comfort with using the technique

■ having convenient data that support the application of a particular technique.

The use of the techniques as described in this book might lead you to circumvent the quality and/or quantity of analysis necessary for formulating and implementing effective competitive strategy for a number of reasons. For example, our experience suggests that it is far too easy to draw incorrect conclusions from incomplete or defective data with a number of these techniques. As mentioned earlier, the quality of the data is critical to the effective delivery of analytical outputs.

You should also note that in spite of the presence of a very broad range of analytical techniques, a few of which we describe in this book, some organisations may still adopt poor decisions. Researchers have identified a variety of common cognitive biases that can enter into the process of analysis. These include:

■ *Escalating commitment.* This is where executives commit more and more resources to a project even when they receive evidence that it is failing. The more rational move would be to 'cut one's losses and run', but rationality is often overcome in these cases by feelings of personal responsibility, an inability to admit one's error, or a failure to acknowledge changes in the assumptions that supported the initial decision.

■ *'Groupthink'.* This occurs when a group of decision makers (for example, a senior management team) embarks on a poorly determined course of action without thoroughly questioning the underlying assumptions of the decision. It is often based on an emotional rather than an objective assessment of the appropriate course of action and is most prevalent in organisations with strong leadership and cultures.

■ *Illusion of control.* This is an individual's tendency to overestimate their ability to control events. For example, someone who has had an ongoing string of picking winning lottery tickets might come to think that they are better at it than they truly are. This is often the result of overconfidence, and senior executives have been shown to be particularly prone to this bias.

■ *The prior hypothesis bias.* Individuals who have strong beliefs about the relationships between variables tend to make decisions on the basis of these beliefs even when presented with analytical evidence that contradicts them. Additionally, these individuals often seek and use data only when they confirm their beliefs, while ignoring data that contradict them. In strategic terms, this may happen when the top executive has a strong belief that the organisation's existing strategy makes sense and continues to pursue it despite the evidence that shows it is inappropriate.

■ *Simplification.* This is where individuals use simple examples to make sense out of not so simple problems. Oversimplifying complex problems is dangerous and can mislead an organisation into making bad decisions. This is one of the key cautions we make in applying the techniques contained in this book.

■ *Representativeness.* This is a bias that violates the statistical law of large numbers in that individuals often display a tendency to generalise from small samples (such as their experience) to explain a larger phenomena or population.

The existence of these biases raises questions as to the analytical process and its purpose and outcomes. People in organisations often tend to collect more information than strictly necessary for decision making, partly to influence others and partly to be seen as 'rational'. In other words, analysis is often used not just for objective decision making but also for political purposes.

In fact, formal analysis would be less necessary if people could execute their decisions themselves and nobody had to convince anybody of anything.

Because of these issues and related problems, these techniques should never be used to circumvent the strategic thinking necessary to gain a thorough understanding of an organisation's business and competitive environment today or where it should be in the future. They will help improve strategic thinking but are not a replacement for it.

What does it take to successfully perform analysis? There is a number of 'competencies' that someone undertaking analysis should demonstrate. One of the better summaries of these competencies comes from the Society of Competitive Intelligence Professionals (SCIP), which suggest the following:

■ recognise the interaction between the collection and analysis stages

- use creativity
- employ both deductive and inductive reasoning
- use alternative thinking
- understand the basic analytical models
- introduce exciting and attractive models to elicit the discovery notion of analysis rather than the dry, research approach
- know when and why to use the various analysis tools
- recognise the inevitable existence of gaps and blind spots
- know when to cease analysing so as to avoid analysis paralysis.

There are literally hundreds of strategic, tactical and operational analysis techniques that we could have included in this book. Instead, we have extensively reviewed the literature in the field and considered survey research and our own experiences in determining those we view as potentially being the most applicable across a broad range of applications in the analysis process.

As outlined in Chapter 1, this book examines 12 so-called 'classic' techniques involved in analysing business and competitive data and information, including environmental analysis, industry analysis, competitor analysis and organisational analysis models. It will help any businessperson to draw effective conclusions from limited data and to put together information that does not often fit together at first glance.

You should also be alert to the fact that any listing of techniques is bound to run into a variety of problems of semantics and definitional confusion. Some of the techniques included in this book are known by multiple names. This might have occurred because the technique came to be associated with a particular originating organisation (for example, the BCG matrix), a particular author (Porter's five forces model is an example) or has retained a generic nomenclature (perhaps competitor analysis). We recognise that some of the techniques included in this book have seen modifications in use over the years or are derivatives of other closely related techniques. In all cases, we have tried to include and describe the most popularly known versions of the techniques as opposed to all of a technique's possible derivatives. We have tried to alert you to where there is overlap between techniques by referring you to the supporting techniques within the text.

We must also note that it is not our intention to 'reinvent the wheel' when it comes to the analytical techniques. The techniques included herein all have a history. This book's techniques have been and are in use in real organisations – they do not exist just in theory.

Analysis tools

3

BCG growth/share portfolio matrix

Description and purpose

Portfolio planning BCG matrix models are designed to help the analyst better understand the attractiveness or potential of a portfolio of distinct business units in a multi-unit business. They developed from two areas: the planning department at General Electric (GE) and the Boston Consulting Group (BCG). GE is generally credited with being the first to present a comprehensive portfolio matrix in the early 1960s.

Shortly after the initial developments at GE, BCG took the business world by storm with the introduction of its growth/share portfolio matrix (BCG matrix). Its intuitive appeal and vivid imagery combined with the appearance of good quantitative analysis caught the interest of many strategic planners searching for a legitimate tool to manage diversified multi-unit corporate strategy.

The BCG matrix was designed to help managers of multiproduct, multi-market, multinational businesses assess their corporate level strategy by:

- providing them with an analytical framework to determine the optimal product or business portfolio
- prescribing a set of strategies to guide resource allocation across the portfolio
- providing them with a framework for analysing competing business portfolios.

The BCG matrix allows a multibusiness company to evaluate the merits of its individual business units or business lines to determine appropriate market strategies for each business. The business portfolios are evaluated using a common measuring stick based on the attractiveness of the industry in which they compete and their relative competitive position. Generic strategies are then recommended depending on the position of the individual business unit or line in the portfolio matrix.

Crafting a fit between the organisation's goals, capabilities and the environment in which it operates is at the core of strategic planning. The tactical delivery of strategic planning is the allocation of resources to competing internal opportunities. This is a challenging task for focused companies, but it can quickly spiral into unmanageable complexity for a diversified company.

The BCG matrix integrated two previously established management theories: the experience curve and the product life cycle.

Link to the experience curve

BCG found that per unit costs often decrease as output levels increase due to the impact of experience. Experience is composed of three functions: learning, specialisation and scale.

- The *learning function* shows that anyone doing a job learns to do it better over time.

- The *specialisation function* shows that by dividing jobs into individual tasks, each employee's experience with the task increases, and costs decline because of the increased learning.

- The *scale function* suggests that the capital costs required to finance additional capacity diminish as that capacity grows.

The sequential impact of these three functions on profitability is shown in Figure 3.1.

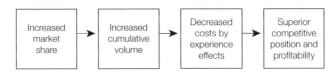

Figure 3.1 Experience curve sequence

Based on this logical sequence, a major strategic implication was drawn from experience curve theory: the company capturing the largest market share achieves the highest accumulated volume, achieving a superior competitive position due to cost reductions from the experience curve effect.

Link to the product life cycle

The other building block of the BCG growth matrix was the well-established concept of the product life cycle (PLC). The product life cycle was selected as the natural complement to the experience curve based on the following chain of logic.

If market share is the surest road to higher accumulated volumes and subsequent lower costs and higher profitability, then the company's resources are best spent pursuing high growth markets.

The surest route to maximise total company profitability is to maximise market share across the strategic business unit (SBU) or business line (SBL) portfolio. The best way to accomplish this is to transfer profits or resources away from the mature and declining products to the introductory and growth products of the PLC. The relevant assumptions of the PLC are twofold:

■ Market share is easier to secure in high-growth markets because competitive retaliation is less severe when it is secured through new growth instead of taking it from competitors. It is also easier to secure because new consumers or users have lower branding preference relative to experienced ones.

■ Products in the mature stage of the life cycle generate excess cash, whereas products in the growth stage require or absorb more cash.

Combining the experience curve and the product life cycle

The BCG matrix in Figure 3.2 is the result of the integration of experience curve and PLC theory.

The BCG matrix plots market attractiveness (measured by market growth as derived from PLC theory) and competitive position (measured by market share as derived from experience curve theory) to compare the situation of different products or SBUs. Market attractiveness is measured by the industry's growth rate, whereas competitive position is measured by the business unit's market share relative to that of its largest competitor in the industry (as opposed to the market as a whole). For example, if a business unit has a market share of 20 per cent and its largest competitor has a market share of 40 per cent, then the business unit's relative market share is 0.5. The purpose of this comparison is to define an appropriate market strategy for each business unit.

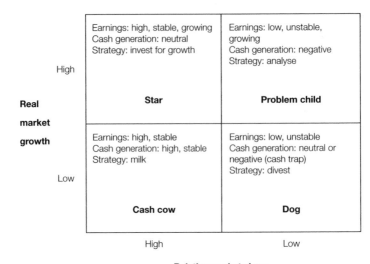

Figure 3.2 The BCG growth matrix

The overall strategy of the multibusiness company, as suggested by the BCG matrix, is to maximise market share in as many high-growth markets for as many SBUs/SBLs as possible. The upper limit of this possibility is limited by cash flow because the model assumes an internal cash balance between cash use and cash generation. Hence, the strategic goal for senior executives is to allocate limited cash resources across the business units or lines to maximise company profitability.

Each quadrant in the BCG matrix offers generic strategies to achieve maximum profitability under this constraint.

Stars – high growth rate, high market share

The high growth rate of stars requires a heavy cash investment. Their strong market share position infers that stars move furthermost along the experience curve. Therefore, stars should soon develop high margins, resulting in potentially strong cash flows in the near future and, hence, a sustainable cash position. Application of the BCG matrix presumes that stars will eventually become cash cows. It recommends that if stars are cash-deficient, they should be supported with the investment necessary to maintain their market share; and if they are cash providers, the surplus should be reinvested.

Cash cows – low growth rate, high market share

Products or SBUs in mature markets require lower cash investments and, therefore, will provide cash flow from which to finance businesses in other more promising quadrants. The BCG matrix suggests that cash cows be 'milked' by a strategy that only invests in maintaining their current positions. Excess cash flow should be reinvested in either stars or selected problem children.

Dogs – low growth rate, low market share

The low growth rate of dogs infers that increasing their market share will be a costly proposition. Additionally, their low market share implies an uncompetitive cost structure by virtue of their inferior position on the experience curve. Hence, dogs are unprofitable and usually require heavy cash investments just to maintain their low market share. An application of the BCG matrix recommends three options for dogs:

- they can become profitable with a focused strategy on a specific desired niche or segment
- any further investment can be withheld while 'milking' them for any cash that they can still generate
- they can be divested or slowly put to sleep.

Problem children – high growth rate, low market share

The high growth rate of problem children requires a heavy cash investment. An intensifying factor is their low market share, which implies an uncompetitive cost structure by virtue of their inferior position on the experience curve. As the maturity stage sets in, the problem child follows one of two paths on the matrix:

- if market share cannot be grown, the problem child will become a dog
- alternately, if market share can be increased by a high enough amount, the problem child will be exalted into star status and eventually become a cash cow.

The BCG matrix recommends that the most promising problem children should receive cash investments to increase their market share, but those problem children with dismal prospects should not receive further cash investment.

The integration of these classifications and their requisite strategies are shown in Figure 3.3 (the numbers indicate strategic priority).

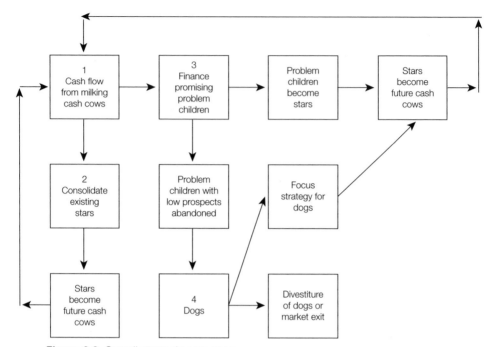

Figure 3.3 Overall strategic sequence

Strengths

The simplicity of the BCG matrix may be its greatest strength. It presents a great deal of information in one diagram; the complexities of a multibusiness strategy are seemingly captured in an accessible format. Many other management tools cannot match the depth and breadth of information that this growth/share matrix offers in one concise view. Its straightforwardness allows it to be used easily and quickly to identify areas for further in-depth analysis.

The BCG matrix challenged the status quo that internal investment should be directed on the basis of past performance or should reward managers for past performance. In some respects, the portfolio approach fosters a mindset focused on future demand.

It additionally assists with areas such as the following:

■ *Trend analysis*. Changes in the relative SBU markets can be detected easily through the use of multiperiod matrices.

■ *Competitive analysis*. Determining the strategic progress of competitor companies can be easily facilitated by plotting a time series of competitor matrices.

■ *Easy to communicate.* The matrix and the resulting recommendations are easy for decision makers to understand.

■ *Challenges existing management philosophy.* One of the main strengths of portfolio analysis is the change in perspective that it induces in the minds of its users. It recognises that corporate strategy must be an integration of individual business strategy at the business unit level. This was an improvement on the preceding mindset that tended to apply blanket strategies across the entire multi-unit company and neglected the differences across the various product markets in which it operated. The BCG portfolio approach heightens management's sensitivity by combining corporate level and business level strategy.

Weaknesses

BCG matrix has several limitations. The experience curve link to the BCG matrix may not be relevant to the competitive parameters of a particular product market. Relative market share is not necessarily a good proxy for competitive position (that is, there is not a clear or singular relationship between market share and profitability in all industries).

High market share is not necessarily more profitable than low market share. Many profitable companies have demonstrated that competition in low growth mature markets should not be categorically ruled out as a strategic option. Similarly, the emphasis on market dominance is being constantly challenged by successful niche players who specialise in product or service differentiation.

Market share is assumed to be a dependent variable, whereas market growth is assumed to be an independent variable. This is not necessarily correct. The assumption that market growth rate is a variable beyond the control of management confuses the cause and effect sequence of effective strategy – strategy should lead to growth rather than growth leading to strategy.

The BCG matrix assumes that investment opportunities inside a company are superior to investment opportunities outside the company. The emergence of advanced capital markets, coupled with the difficulty of managing diversity in the absence of specific market knowledge, suggests that portfolio management has become less useful. It is quite possible that increasing dividends or investing surplus cash cow funds in money markets offers a higher rate of return than investing internally in stars and problem children.

Strategic business units sometimes cannot be unambiguously defined. The nature of SBUs with regard to their interrelatedness (such as joint costs, synergy, demand and interdependencies) makes the positioning on the matrix a fruitless exercise in classification.

The characteristics of the product market influence the strategic recommendations offered by the BCG matrix. There is significant room for error in applying the trade-off between operational breadth (to include competitive experience effects) and depth (to allow for meaningful segmentation).

Often, it is valuable for a company to retain dogs to maintain a portfolio of strategic options, such as supply security, a source of competitive intelligence and escape from the onset of entry barriers in certain industries. The benefits of strategic flexibility may supercede profitability, at least for a designated period of time. For example, a strict application of portfolio theory would suggest that most car dealerships would be wise to divest their new car business; however, new car sales are often an important driver for the highly lucrative service segment.

Given that the BCG growth matrix only incorporates the competitive threat to market share from the most dominant competitor, there is a risk of being misled. A rapidly rising competitor may not show up on the BCG radar until it has gained enough market share to become a dominant player in the market.

A further source of bias may be the selection of data and definition by managers seeking to achieve a star label for their particular management domains. The unintended consequences of the BCG matrix may be 'politics' and game playing around these subjective analytical parameters.

While the BCG matrix remains an impressive conceptual framework, it should be primarily used as a starting point for subsequent analysis. When done in conjunction with other analytical tools and techniques, it can help provide a holistic approach to corporate strategy development.

How to do it

True to its systematic nature, the process for using the BCG matrix is sequential and can be generalised into the following steps.

Step 1: Divide the company into its SBUs or business product lines/segments

Divide the company into its economically distinct product market seg-ments or around specific business units. Take care with this first step because the business line's position on the matrix – and hence the strategic recommendations of the model – depend in large part on this initial defi-nition of the product. You are trying to find units that have an established and separate profit and loss (P&L) or budgeting profile.

Common segmentation criteria include similar situational or behavioural characteristics, a discontinuity in growth rates, share patterns, distribution patterns, cross elasticity of substitute products, geography, interdependent prices, similar competition, similar customers served or a potential for shared experience. A common rule of thumb is that a management team can only realistically manage strategies for approximately 30 different busi-ness lines – anything beyond this number becomes unmanageable and counter-productive. As you might imagine, many management teams have struggled with far less than this number!

A great deal of judgement is thus required to determine the extent of seg-mentation within the product market definition. A wide enough scope must be maintained to correctly incorporate competitive opportunities and threats from areas outside of the traditional or intuitive boundaries. Conversely, the definition of an SBU or strategic business line (SBL) must be narrow enough to allow for distinctions fine enough to make the analysis operational. Despite the difficulty of properly defining the individual business lines or units, this process of analysis often offers important strategic insights of its own accord.

Step 2: Measure the growth rate of each SBU or SBL market

A useful percentage growth formula for the market growth rate is:

$$\text{Market growth rate, year}_x = \frac{(\text{market size, year}_x) - (\text{market size, year}_{x-1}) \times 100}{\text{market size, year}_{x-1}}$$

Step 3: Measure the relative market share of each SBU or SBL

Contrary to the formula in Step 2, relative market share is not measured in percentage terms, but as a ratio of the business unit's or business line's market share versus that of its largest competitor.

For example, a market share ratio of 2 shows that the SBU has a relative market share twice that of its next leading competitor. Alternately, a ratio of 0.5 shows that the SBU has a relative market share that is half of that of its leading competitor. Note that normally an SBU will have more than one product, making the use of a weighted average of the individual product growth rates a suitable technique. Either nominal or real sales data may be used. You want an accurate estimate of relative market share; however, you do not need two decimal levels of precision in generating the ratio!

Step 4: Position each SBU or SBL along the matrix dimensions

Plotting on the vertical axis – market growth rate

Simply draw a threshold point to distinguish SBUs or SBLs that are experiencing fast growth from those that are gaining market share slowly. The BCG matrix uses the average growth rate for the market as this horizontal line of demarcation. Alternately, a corporate target may be used to define this threshold. Consistent with the product life cycle, products that lie above this line are considered to be in the growth stage. Products or business lines below this line are considered to be in either the maturity or decline stage of the product life cycle.

Plotting on the horizontal axis – relative market share

Experience curve theory asserts that market share is related to total accumulated volume, which is the major factor driving down costs through the experience curve effect. Plot relative market share on a semi-log scale. A semi-log graph or plot is a way of visualising data that are exponentially changing. One axis is plotted on a logarithmic scale.

A cut-off point also needs to be established on the horizontal axis with regard to both high and low market share. The BCG matrix recommends this vertical line of demarcation to be a relative market share of 1.0. Any relative market share to the right of 1.0 indicates the threshold of competitive strength in that market.

Plot contribution bubbles

The two cut-off points (high versus low growth and high versus low market share) allow the graph to be divided into the characteristic four quadrants of the BCG matrix. Plotting the growth rate versus relative market share will only give pinpoint locations on the matrix. A helpful technique is to plot bubbles around these points to indicate the relative size of each SBU/SBL in terms of its contribution to total company sales or profitability.

$$\text{Relative size of bubble} = \frac{\text{SBU sales or profitability}}{\text{Total firm sales or profitability}}$$

Sales volume is generally the preferred method of determining the size of the bubbles for several reasons: it is easier to make a comparison to competition (see Step 5); competitor profit figures by SBU/SBL are difficult to obtain; and internal profit figures are often distorted by arbitrary allocations. Each bubble should also be labelled using a common convention, such as numerical or alphabetical order, for further referencing.

Upon determining each unit's placement within the matrix, the following predictions can be made: the size, stability and growth potential of the future earnings of each business unit or line; and the cash flow that each business should provide.

The intermediate analytical product of Steps 1 to 4 should look similar to the graph displayed in Figure 3.4.

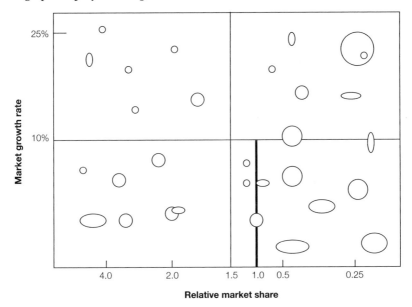

Figure 3.4 Matrix graph

Step 5: Construct a matrix for all competitors

Repeat Steps 1 to 4 to construct matrices for competitor business units or product lines. This will help to give the analysis an external focus on the competitive environment.

Step 6: Assign optimal generic strategies to each business unit or product line

Table 3.1 summarises the appropriate strategies recommended by an application of the BCG matrix after the SBUs/SBLs have been positioned in the matrix. Basically, the strategies can be summarised by the following modes of action: divest the dogs; milk the cash cows; invest in the stars; and analyse the problem child to determine whether it can be grown into a star or will degenerate into a dog.

Table 3.1 Strategies for the BCG matrix

Business category	Market share thrust	Business profitability	Investment required	Net cash flow
Stars	Hold/increase	High	High	Around zero or slightly negative
Cash cows	Hold	High	Low	Highly positive
Problem child (a)	Increase	None or negative	Very high	Highly negative
Problem child (b)	Harvest/divest	Low or negative	Do not invest	Positive
Dogs	Harvest/divest	Low or negative	Do not invest	Positive

Source: Adapted from Hax, A. and Majluf, N.S., 'The use of the growth share matrix in strategic planning', *Interfaces*, February, 1983, 46–60.

Step 7: Further disaggregate the analysis

The matrix approach can be further defined to map out the relative positions of the composite products within each business. This might help with the tactical implementation of Step 6.

Step 8: Introduce analytical dynamics

Steps 1 to 7 result in a static analysis. Two analytical tools can be introduced at this stage to incorporate historical market evolution and sustainable growth rate, as described below.

Construct a share momentum graph

The purpose of a share momentum graph is to plot long-term market growth versus long-term sales to detect which SBUs/SBLs are losing market share despite growing sales. This tool is easy to apply because it uses the same data as the matrix. It serves to highlight important distinctions that may be overlooked by only using the BCG matrix (see Figure 3.5).

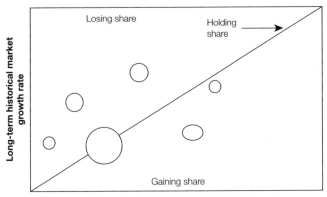

Figure 3.5 Share momentum graph
Source: Adapted from Hax, A. and Majluf, N.S., 'The use of the growth share matrix in strategic planning', *Interfaces*, February, 1983, 52.

Sustainable growth rate analysis

Introduced during the high inflationary era of the 1970s, the BCG matrix assumed that the company's growth would be internally financed. In a lower inflation environment, the sustainable growth rate formula can be used to determine the maximum rate of growth without increasing equity. It is a helpful way to integrate financial strategy with the BCG matrix.

$$g = p \times [\text{ROA} = D/E(\text{ROA} - i)]$$

Where:

g = upper limit on sustainable growth
p = percentage of earnings retained
ROA = tax adjusted return on assets
D = total debt
E = total equity
i = tax adjusted cost of debt

Step 9: Iteration

Repeating Steps 1 to 8 serves two strategic purposes: strategic evaluation and competitive analysis.

Strategic evaluation

The success of the chosen strategies over time can be graphically displayed by overlaying a time series matrix chart to determine if a business unit or business product lines are moving into their desired positions on the matrix. An optimal result would show that problem children increase in both market share and market growth rate to become stars; stars decrease in market growth rate but sustain market share to become cash cows; dogs are either divested or moved into the problem child or star quadrants; and cash cows exhibit stable positions.

Competitive analysis

The progress of rival companies can be monitored by repeating this process with a time series of matrix graphs compiled of competitors and constructing an updated share momentum graph for competitors. Competitive threats and opportunities may reveal themselves with these tools. It has been suggested that the best competitive analysis within a matrix format is the share momentum graphs (see Figure 3.5) because temporary aberrations will not distort the analysis, and cut-off points may change over time.

The broadband cable TV Industry

Over the first decade of the twenty-first century, it is anticipated that the cable industry will become another access technology in the converging markets of telecommunications, broadcasting, Internet and e-commerce. The first signs of this new trend started to appear in the late 1990s. Cable TV operators in the United States upgraded their networks and slowly started to add high-speed Internet services. These were seen as an important step to surpass satellite demand.

For millions of people across the globe, television brings news, entertainment and educational programmes into their homes. Many people now get their TV signals from cable television (CATV) because it provides a clearer picture and more channels. Many people who have cable TV can now also get a high-speed connection (broadband) to the Internet from their cable provider.

Despite the apparent growth opportunities, the broadband cable industry has experienced financial difficulty. As part of a study to examine the status and strategies of this industry on a worldwide basis, a BCG matrix was used to identify the nature of the products offered. The positioning of the 'products' of the broadband cable industry into a BCG matrix was undertaken, with the results identified in Figure 3.6.

From this BCG matrix, the following conclusions could be drawn at a global level:

- The telephony services – the dog – should be reviewed and consideration be given as to whether or not to discontinue them.

- The cable TV service – the cash cow – should be managed on a cost-conscious basis to deliver the maximum positive cash flow.

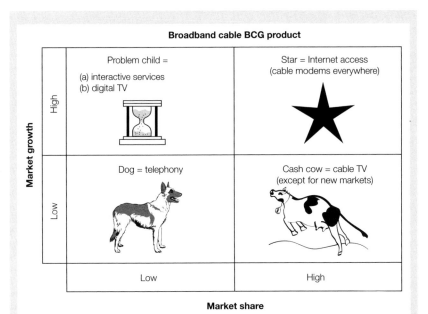

Broadband cable BCG product

Figure 3.6 Broadband cable BCG product portfolio

■ The cash flow from the cable TV service would be used to support the continued growth of the Internet access service – the star – and to promote the development of the new interactive services – the problem child – any one of which could possibly become the growth star of the future.

■ Interactive services – the problem child – are closely coupled with the deployment of digital TV, where the intention is to provide them on a TV set. Otherwise they could be supported through Internet access services using a PC. However, they would then become part of the electronic commerce Internet world, and the ability of the broadband cable company to add value (and thereby derive additional revenue) would be extremely limited.

The fundamental issue of how the choice between TV and PC will be resolved – or more realistically, how the two will be merged within a home network – might well decide the next star service.

Source: Adapted from McGrail, M. and Roberts, B., 'Strategies in the broadband cable TV industry: the challenges for management and technology innovation', *Info*, 7(1), 2005, 53–65.

4

Competitor analysis

Description and purpose

The purpose of competitor analysis is to provide a comprehensive picture of the strengths and weaknesses of current and potential competitors to identify opportunities and threats for your organisation. The four main objectives of competitor analysis are as follows:

- identify competitors' future plans and strategies
- predict competitors' likely reactions to competitive initiatives
- determine the match between a competitor's strategy and its capabilities
- understand a competitor's weaknesses.

Professor Michael Porter from Harvard University was one of the first strategists to propose a formal and systematic model to gather information about competitors (see Figure 4.1). This model encourages you to use current and past information about competitors to predict the future strategic moves that a competitor may pursue in response to the company's own strategies, the strategies of other companies in the industry, or broad changes in the competitive environment external to business strategies. This puts you in a superior position to craft strategies for both attack and defence.

The rationale for competitor analysis is simple – a superior knowledge of competitors offers a legitimate source of competitive advantage. The essence of competitive advantage consists of offering superior customer value in the company's chosen market. Customer value is defined relative

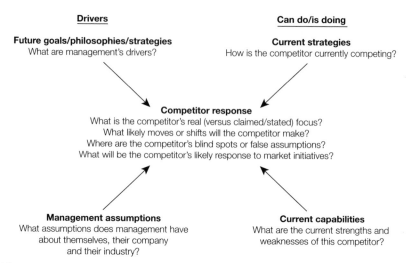

Figure 4.1 The components of competitor analysis
Source: Adapted from Porter, M.E., *Competitive Strategy: Techniques for Analyzing Industries and Competitors* (New York: The Free Press, 1980).

to competitor offerings, making competitor knowledge an intrinsic component of corporate strategy.

Competitor analysis facilitates the objective of achieving superior customer value in three important ways:

- first, it can reveal strategic weaknesses in competitors to exploit

- second, its proactive stance will allow the company to anticipate the response of their competitors to its planned strategies, the strategies of other competing companies and changes in the environment

- third, this knowledge will give the company strategic agility.

An attacking strategy can be implemented more quickly to capitalise on your strengths and exploit opportunities. Similarly, a defensive strategy can be employed more deftly to counter the threat of competitor companies from exploiting your company's weaknesses.

Clearly, companies practising systematic and advanced competitor analysis and profiling have a significant advantage. As such, a comprehensive profiling capability is becoming a core competence required for successful business competition.

Strengths

In addition to the advantages just outlined, there are several other related benefits:

- competitor analysis encourages your company to adopt a confident, aggressive and proactive position toward competitive strategy and the broader business environment

- the knowledge provided about competitors allows your company to help shape and define the parameters of strategy rather than react to unexpected competitive sideswipes

- the inclusive nature of competitor analysis encourages the sharing of insights and perspectives across functional boundaries of the company. Many opportunities are often uncovered that otherwise would have remained hidden

- it creates an efficient and effective approach to strategy formulation. The relevant, timely, concise and visually accessible presentation formats of this technique are an excellent vehicle to communicate strategy.

Weaknesses

The primary criticism of competitor analysis relates to the temptation for companies to make it the cornerstone of their competitive strategy. In attempting to become an industry leader, a company will eventually become a follower if it defines leadership too closely in respect to current competitors because

- comparisons to competitors must always relate to the notion of customer value

- constantly referencing a company's strategy to competitors will eventually blind a company to innovative approaches of potential new competitors from outside the periphery of the industry who deliver superior customer value. Thus, it is important to keep an eye on potential new competitors from seemingly unrelated sectors and industries.

The copycat nature of outpacing the competition may prevent any competitive advantage from becoming sustainable – companies should focus on generating real customer value, not 'me-too' imitation, in their search for profitable innovation.

How to do it

There are seven steps in the competitor analysis process:

1 Determine who your competitors are.

2 Determine who your potential competitors may be.

3 Decide what information you need about these competitors.

4 Conduct a competitor analysis of the gathered information.

5 Present your insights to decision makers in an appropriate format and in a timely manner.

6 Develop a strategy based on the analysis.

7 Continually monitor competitors and scan for potential competitors.

Steps 1 and 2: Determine who your competitors are and who they may be in the future

The first two steps are closely related. Your competitors include those companies that serve the same customer base as you. However, what is your customer base? Is it customers of the same product or customers of the same product category? Ultimately, all companies are competitors in that they are all trying to attract the same discretionary income. Although this last delineation may sound extreme, it underscores the importance of including potential competitors at the beginning of the analysis. Given the factors of industry changes and value chain erosion, it is important to include potential new competitors at the outset to prevent the analysis from becoming too narrowly focused.

There are two ways to define competitors:

■ *The traditional method.* More adept at identifying current competitors, this method focuses on defining strategic groups within industries. Strategic groups are closely related companies with relatively similar strategies, occupying similar links on the industry's value chain and sharing similar resource capabilities.

■ *The less obvious method.* This focuses on identifying potential new competitors who are not yet visible. They are developing new ways of delivering customer value on new competitive platforms and are often unaware of the companies they will soon supplant. By focusing on customer value, and the question 'Which competitors do your customers see as *your* major competition?' companies can define potential competitors according to their provision of comparable customer value through different platforms, for both products and services. Focus on defining potential competitors based on changing customer tastes and preferences, motivations, product or service deployment, or technological innovation.

Generally, the most valuable sources of information regarding the identification of both current and potential competitors will be your company's own customers, sales staff, marketing representatives and operations managers – in other words, those who interact the most with customers. Other less valuable sources may be found in industry directories, trade association materials and other secondary information resources.

Step 3: Decide what information you need about these competitors

Start this step with the internal end user of the output of your analysis – the strategic decision makers within your company. They will be in the best position to itemise exactly what types of competitor information would be most beneficial. To facilitate this objective, focus information gathering on the strategic needs of the decision makers.

Table 4.1 depicts the types and categories of information that may be considered during this stage.

You can get ideas about useful types and sources of information from surveys and benchmarking studies. However, information needs will be largely industry-specific or even company-specific and will change over time.

Table 4.1 Typical categories and types of competitor profile information

Background information	Products/services	Marketing
■ Name	■ Number of products/services	■ Segmentation strategies
■ Location		
■ Short description	■ Diversity or breadth of product lines	■ Branding and image
■ History	■ Quality, embedded customer value	■ Probable growth vectors
■ Key events		
■ Major transactions	■ Projected new products/services	■ Advertising/ promotions
■ Ownershp structure	■ Current market shares	■ Market research capability

Background information	*Products/services*	*Marketing*
	by product and product line	▓ Customer service emphasis
	▓ Projected market shares	▓ 4 P parameters – product, price, promotion, place
		▓ Key customers

Human resources	*Operations*	*Management profiles*
▓ Quality and skill of personnel	▓ Manufacturing capacity	▓ Personality
▓ Turnover rates	▓ Ability to mass customise	▓ Background
▓ Labour costs	▓ Cycle time, manufacturing agility and flexibility	▓ Motivations, aspirations
▓ Level of training		▓ Style
▓ Flexibility	▓ TQM implementation	▓ Past successes and failures
▓ Union relations	▓ Overhead costs	▓ Depth of managerial talent
	▓ Lean production methods	

Sociopolitical	*Technology*	*Organisational structure*
▓ Government contacts	▓ Process technology	▓ Nature of hierarchy
▓ Stakeholder reputation	▓ R&D expertise	▓ Team building
▓ Breadth and depth of portfolio of sociopolitical assets	▓ Proprietary technology, patents, copyrights	▓ Cross functionality
	▓ Information and communication infrastructure	▓ Major ownership
▓ Public affairs experience		▓ Cultural alignment
▓ Nature of government contracts	▓ Ability to internally innovate	
▓ Connections of board members	▓ Access to outside expertise through licensing, alliances, joint ventures	
▓ Issue and crisis management capacity		

CI capacity	Strategy	Customer value analysis
■ Evidence of formal CI capacity	■ Positioning	■ Quality attributes
■ Reporting relationships	■ Future plans	■ Service attributes
■ Profile	■ Mission and vision	■ Customer goals and motivations
■ CEO and top management level of support	■ Goals, objectives	■ Customer types and numbers
■ Vulnerability	■ Corporate portfolio	■ Net worth (benefits minus costs) of ownership
■ Integration	■ Synergies	
■ Data gathering and analysis assets	■ Resources/capabilities	
	■ Core competencies	
	■ Strengths and weaknesses	

Financial
■ Financial statements
■ Securities filings
■ Absolute and comparative ratio analysis
■ Disaggregated ratio analysis
■ Cash flow analysis
■ Sustainable growth rate
■ Stock performance
■ Costs

Contrary to intuition, most of the information required for this step already exists inside your company; that is, salespeople, marketing staff, operations and probably everyone in the company is in possession of valuable nuggets of competitive information. Figuring prominently in these primary sources of competitive information are your company's own customers and suppliers.

Step 4: Conduct a competitor analysis of the gathered information

Porter's framework depicted in Figure 4.1 can be used as a guide when analysing the gathered information, as follows:

■ *Future goals*. Determining the future goals of your competitors will help to forecast their strategies and identify strategies for your company. To understand where a competitor is headed, identify its market share, profitability and organisational performance. Also try to discover what has been stated by its key spokespeople with regard to its future direction – how does it claim to see itself operating in the future?

■ *Current strategy*. First, determine which of the three strategies (low cost, differentiation or focus) the company is pursuing. A current strategy may be identified on the basis of both what it says and what it does.

Next, identify the strategic implications for each functional area of the competitor's business. Functional areas of the business would include marketing, sales, operations, administration, manufacturing, research and development, finance or personnel.

What are its stated short-term goals? Start by identifying the differences between its future goals and what it is currently doing. Is there synergy and does it make sense, or will it require a major shift to achieve its long-term goals? Are its short-term activities in line with its future goals? Remember, in the absence of particular forces for change, it can be assumed that a company will continue to compete in the future in the same way it has competed in the past.

■ *Capabilities*. Use the information gathered in the current strategy previously to identify what the competitor is doing and what it has the capacity to do. This is about the capacity, skills and resources to actually deliver both its current strategies and future goals. Although a competitor might have announced its strategic intentions, its current capabilities may not enable it to realise them, thus raising questions about the internal thinking of the company.

■ *Assumptions*. A competitor's competitive assumptions about itself, the industry and other competitors yields many useful insights regarding potentially incorrect assumptions or blind spots. Often these blind spots offer competitive opportunities, and this is the crux of the analysis. What assumptions does the competitor hold about its world, and are these reflected in its strategies, both current and future? Assumptions can be identified by the mismatch between capabilities, current strategies and future goals. On the other hand, a company that has all three areas in sync may be a formidable competitor. However, all companies hold assumptions about the world and the future, and they need to be uncovered.

The critical issue underlying competitor analysis is in your understanding of the key assumptions made by the competition. These assumptions may allow you to identify fundamental weaknesses in how they compete and how they see their marketplaces. Answering questions such as 'Are they satisfied with this position?', 'What are their plans?' and 'What are their vulnerabilities?' can provide the necessary understanding to take competitors on.

The four analyses are then integrated into a competitor profile. The purpose is to forecast, with reasonable accuracy, how a competitor will respond to various competitive pressures.

First, determine the attack position of competitors to predict moves they may initiate. Second, determine the defensive position of competitors to forecast how they might react to various competitive pressures.

In making these determinations, qualitative factors may often outweigh quantitative factors.

Step 5: Present your analytical insights to decision makers in an appropriate format and in a timely manner

Visual depictions are more effective than written reports. We consider three types of formatting schemes:

- *Comparison grid*. Plot competitor positions (performance, capabilities, key success factor and so on) on high/low dependent and independent variable cross-hair axes. Depending on the application, the company's performance or industry averages are used as the point of reference. Comparison grids provide good snapshots of relative performance across two competitive parameters (see Figure 4.2).

- *Radar chart*. Simple to comprehend yet dense with information, radar charts are often used to communicate profiling analysis. Radar charts are composed of an underlying circle with several points on the circumference representing industry averages around relative competitive parameters. Superimposed over these circles are geometric shapes representing the performance of the company or competitor being analysed. The resulting geometric overlay will depict a concise visual of relative performance, whether it be superior or inferior performance (see Figure 4.3).

- *Visual competitor strength grid*. Competitor strength grids are a simple yet effective way of depicting the relative superiority between

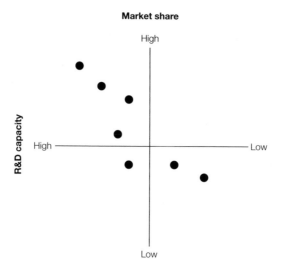

Figure 4.2 Comparison grid

Figure 4.3 Radar charts

competitor companies along any number of competitive parameters. By assigning a spectrum of colours (or symbols) to represent relative competitive inferiority, parity and superiority, the graph depicts the spectrum of relative competitive advantage among competitors (see Table 4.2).

These charts and similar visual depictions will facilitate brainstorming sessions during the strategy development process.

Given the rapidity of environmental and competitive change, competitor intelligence has value only if it is received in a timely fashion by the relevant strategic decision makers. In this respect, timeliness and relevance supersede complete accuracy.

Table 4.2 Visual competitor strength grid (for pizza delivery restaurants in Southern Ontario)

Key success factors	Armando's	Domino's	Little Caesar's	Pizza Hut	Pizza King	Pizza Pizza
1 Breadth of product offering	<	>	<	★	•	>
2 Geographic coverage	•	★	>	>	<	<
3 Name recognition	•	★	>	>	<	<
4 Product quality	★	<	•	<	>	>
5 Production & delivery reliability	<	>	★	>	•	<
6 Supply chain management	<	>	★	>	•	<

Guide: ★ best in class | > above average | < below average | • worst in class

Step 6: Develop strategy based on the analysis

At this point, competitor profiles used to develop strategy around several relevant competitive considerations, such as:

■ determining the probable rules of engagement within that strategic position

■ choosing the arena or scope of engagement – where, how and against whom your company will compete

■ developing a strategy that leverages your company's strengths, exploits competitors' weaknesses, neutralises competitive threats and defends against weaknesses.

Choose strategies that will force competitors to make costly strategic trade-offs, should they decide to impinge on your strategy.

Step 7: Continually monitor competitors and scan for potential competitors

Always assume that competitors are simultaneously performing similar analysis on your company. This is reason enough to engage in continual monitoring. Volatile markets, hyper-competition, industry migration and decoupled value chains give ample rationale for the continual monitoring of current *and* potential competitors.

As mentioned throughout this chapter, the key goal of competitor analysis is to understand how competitors might react to your company's actions and how you can influence competitor behaviour to your company's advantage. Objectives and assumptions are what drive a competitor, and strategy and capabilities are what a competitor is doing or is capable of doing. How can you really understand competitor behaviour? Think of competitor analysis (refer to Figure 4.1) as having four distinct boxes:

Box 1 = future strategies/goals/philosophies

Box 2 = current strategies

Box 3 = current capabilities and resources

Box 4 = management assumptions

The analysis occurs with the comparison of information (Step 3) in Boxes 1, 2 and 3.

A company with managers who understand their competitive environment and have a clearly thought-out growth strategy will find that Boxes 1, 2 and 3 match and are cohesive. This suggests that management's assumptions (Box 4) are minimal and that the company is a formidable competitor.

If Boxes 1, 2 and 3 do not match, you must understand what assumptions are driving management – that is, Box 4. By understanding management's assumptions, you can understand the drivers of this competitor's behaviour.

This can best be explained by the following example.

Chinese mobile market

A competitor analysis was undertaken of a player in the Chinese mobile phone market. Briefly the following sample information was identified:

Future strategies/goals/ philosophies (Box 1)	Current strategies (Box 2)
To be the number one global player in mobile phones.	To offer the lowest price mobile phones.
Management assumptions (Box 4)	**Current capabilities and resources (Box 3)**
That the Chinese government would continue to provide additional funding as required.	The company had substantial financial burdens and, based on its current financial situation, would be unable to repay its debts.

The key pieces of information in Boxes 1, 2 and 3 show there is a mismatch between them – that is, how can a competitor be a global player offering the lowest price phones when they cannot repay their existing debts? Thus a key assumption is operating within the company. This assumption relates to a cultural driver that may no longer necessarily be valid, and it opens up an opportunity for another competitor to offer to buy certain parts of the company, thereby reducing its debt and reliance on the government for additional funding.

While this example provides a brief overview of the technique, when collecting information for Boxes 1, 2 and 3, it is important that you cover the breadth and depth of each facet, as explained by the following scenarios:

■ *Future strategies/goals/philosophies*. A competitor that is focused on reaching short-term financial goals might not be willing to spend much money in response to a competitive attack. Rather, it might favour focusing on the products it can defend. On the other hand, a company that has no short-term profitability objectives might be willing to participate in destructive price competition in which neither company earns a profit.

Competitors' goals commonly include financial issues, growth rate, market share and technology leadership. Goals may be associated with each hierarchical level of strategy – corporate, business unit and functional level.

The competitor's organisational structure provides clues as to which functions are deemed to be the more important. For example, functions that report directly to the CEO are likely to be given priority over those that report to a senior vice president.

Other aspects of the competitor that serve as indicators of its objectives include risk tolerance, management incentives, backgrounds of the executives, composition of the board of directors, legal or contractual restrictions, and any additional corporate-level goals that may influence the competing business unit.

Whether the competitor is meeting its objectives provides an indication of how likely it is to change its strategy.

■ *Current strategies*. The two main indicators about a competitor's strategy are what it says and what it does. What a competitor is saying about its strategy is revealed in

- ■ annual shareholder reports
- ■ financial reports
- ■ interviews with analysts
- ■ statements by managers
- ■ press releases.

However, the stated strategy often differs from what a competitor actually is doing, which will be evident in where its cash flow is directed, such as in the following actions:

- ■ hiring activity
- ■ R&D projects
- ■ capital investments
- ■ marketing campaigns
- ■ strategic partnerships or alliances

- mergers and acquisitions.

- *Current capabilities and resources.* Knowledge of a competitor's objectives and current strategy is useful in understanding how it might want to respond to a competitive attack. However, its resources and capabilities will determine its ability to respond effectively.

A competitor's capabilities can be analysed according to its strengths and weaknesses in various functional areas. Analysis can be taken further to evaluate a competitor's ability to increase its capabilities in certain areas. A financial analysis can also be performed to reveal a company's sustainable growth rate.

Because the competitive environment is dynamic, you need to know about the competitor's ability to react swiftly to change. Factors that slow a company down include low cash reserves, large investments in fixed assets, and an organisational structure that hinders quick action.

- *Management's assumptions.* The assumptions that a competitor's management holds about their company and their industry will help to define their moves. For example, if a player in the industry has introduced a new type of product that failed, other industry players may assume that there is no market for the product. Such assumptions are not always accurate and, if incorrect, may present opportunities. For example, new entrants might have the opportunity to introduce a product similar to a previously unsuccessful one without retaliation because incumbent companies may not take their threat seriously. Honda was able to enter the US motorcycle market with a small motorcycle because US manufacturers, based on their past experience, assumed that there was no market for small motorcycles.

A competitor's assumptions may be based on a number of factors, including any of the following:

- beliefs about its competitive position and other competitors

- past experience with a product or service

- regional factors

- industry trends

- corporate cultural history.

The outcome of competitor analysis is the development of a response profile of possible moves that might be made by a competitor. This profile includes both potential attacking and defensive moves. The ultimate objective of competitor analysis is an improved ability to predict competitors' behaviour – and even to influence that behaviour to a company's advantage.

5

Driving forces analysis

Description and purpose

Driving forces analysis (DFA) is a way of understanding and accounting for change at the industry level. 'Drivers' are clusters of trends that create influences on changes to an industry's structure and a rival's competitive conduct.

So what are driving forces (DFs)? There are forces in every situation that cause things to remain as they are or to change. Forces that push towards change are called 'driving' or 'helping' forces. Forces that resist change are called 'restraining' or 'hindering' forces. When these forces are balanced, no change is likely to occur. When the net effect of these forces is altered and moves away from balance, change occurs in either a helpful or obstructive manner.

Change is not the only factor associated with DFs that firms need to take into account; uncertainty, direction and magnitude (amplitude) are other key elements that a firm must confront as it makes decisions and develops strategies.

The term 'force' refers to the broad cluster of events, state of affairs and, trends that impact the firm's future. DFs are those significant, underlying 'currents' that define and drive events and trends in certain directions. These forces are typically quite broad in scope, long term in nature, and associated with some degree of uncertainty as to their evolution. Examples of DFs include global population growth, institutional commitments to free markets and global trade, advancing use of technology associated with the Internet, and changes in the global climate.

Understanding the DFs is the first step toward establishing a framework for analysing critical trends, particularly as they may impact the competitive environment facing an industry. Industry conditions change because forces are driving industry participants (competitors, customers or suppliers) and related stakeholders (public policy makers, advocacy groups) to alter their actions.

As a result, DFA plays a critical role in the larger strategy development process. DFs indicate the external factors likely to have greatest impact on a firm in the near future. A firm must proactively then address these forces if it is to achieve success.

Strengths

DFA is an essential component of several other analytical techniques, including environment and industry analysis. DFA requires you to take into account the macroenvironment that influences key industry or customer factors likely to impact your firm. For example, government regulations describing the nature of potential entrants or existing players might influence future competition, but there are also many less-obvious external factors

DFs by nature imply change. Change is often the source of competitive advantages for astute industry competitors. Understanding them and their impacts requires managers to consider how conditions will evolve in and around their industries and to consider these forces in their decisions and strategy.

DFA tends to receive a higher than average degree of managerial agreement – particularly when they are involved in the consensus process used for identifying and developing the driving forces. Senior managers often have insights developed over time that can provide valuable perspectives in the DFA process. The inclusion of managers and decision makers in the DF identification and prioritisation process can be a valuable part of getting everyone in the firm focused on the type of strategic thinking and competitive learning that tends to serve firms well in the long run.

DFA can be done in a less data-intense fashion than many other techniques and doesn't necessarily require the firm to gather data on a continual basis as many other analytical techniques do. Data gathering underlying DFA can also be easily supported through the skilled use of data gathering over the Internet. The use of brainstorming, popular group consensus methods and participative technology facilitates its achievement, and it can be done on a less-frequent basis than required for many other tools while still being highly effective.

Weaknesses

DFA cannot drive strategy formulation alone. It seldom specifically answers clients' strategy questions. There are other steps that need to be performed before determining organisational actions (that is, strategies or tactics) even after gaining agreement on DFs. In other words, just recognising and agreeing upon a critical driving force does not tell decision makers what they need to do, but it does tell them that this driving force will impact their future, and that the decisions or strategies that need to be developed must take these impacts into account.

DFs tend to be outside the control of any single organisation to change. What can be done is to change how the firm's strategy or tactics takes them into account. Firms do not manage the DFs, but instead must manage their own responses to them.

The process used to perform DFA nearly always needs to be inclusive and participative. This can be a problem in some firms where key personnel are not available to participate or lack the time to give the necessary consideration to the DF development and prioritisation process. Some firms have experienced difficulties in generating agreements on the DFs or their prioritisation, but this is mostly due to organisational structure reasons or internal politics.

DFA can suffer from many of the common internal, organisational biases when they are generated using only internal personnel. This is because internal personnel tend to see the world through the same (potentially distorted) organisational lenses. As such, it is often useful to employ external resources such as skilled consultants, academics or think tank experts to help the group reach consensus around the DFs.

How to do it

There are two essential steps involved in performing DFA, each of which includes a number of sub-elements that need to be properly addressed before moving forward. The primary analytical task in performing DFA is to:

1   Identify what the relevant DFs are – this requires separating the major causes of industry change from less important ones.

2   Assess the impact they will have on the industry – this involves identifying the small number of DFs that are likely to have greatest impact on the industry and the firm over the next few years.

Step 1: Identifying an industry's DFs

The first task in understanding industry evolution is to look for the DFs of the macroenvironment that influence industry structure and competitive behaviour; for example, changing government regulations, judicial pronouncements and regulatory regimes.

There are also less-obvious external factors. Identifying and assessing these fundamental factors is both the starting point and one of the objectives of scenario analysis.

DFs may seem obvious to one person but be hidden to another; therefore, the identification of DFs should be done in a group or team environment. It is helpful to run through this common list of categories of DFs: social forces/demographic developments, technological developments, economic developments and events, political developments and events, and environmental developments.

Some DFs are unique and specific to a particular industry's situation; nevertheless, most DFs cut across broad swaths of the business environment. They are usually identified by the presence of patterns seen as events and trends, or combinations of trends that combine to create a force. Some of the more common DFs across various industries are as follows:

- changes in the long-term industry growth rate
- changes in who buys the product and how it is used
- changing societal concerns, attitudes and lifestyles
- diffusion of expertise across more firms and locations
- election trends, government decisions or shifting regulatory influences
- growing use of the Internet and its applications
- important firms that enter or exit the industry
- increasing globalisation of the industry
- innovation in communication and marketing

■ innovation in processes and products

■ changes in the long-term industry growth rate

■ major changes in customer needs and preferences

■ major changes in production costs and efficiencies

■ prominent changes in uncertainty and business risk

■ technological change and manufacturing process innovation.

So how do you discover an industry's DFs? You should start by removing from the list all those DFs that are not relevant to your industry. For example, if you are a wholesaler or B2B (business to business) firm, you can probably eliminate end-user type forces from the list. After eliminating the obvious ones, determine if there is another driving force that cannot be readily subsumed inside one of those remaining on the list. If the answer is no, then the force should be included.

Another way of trying to understand DFs is to understand how trends (that is, $T_1...T_n$) or events ($E_1...E_n$) relate to one another and a potential driving force. This is shown in Figure 5.1. This process helps you to understand the relationship between trends and events, and to determine the truly independent driving force as opposed to overlapping ones.

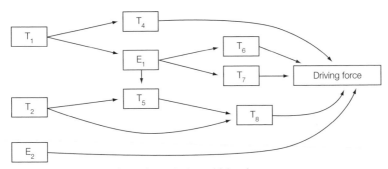

Figure 5.1 Relating trends and events to a driving force

It is a rare analyst or group of managers that can look at their first list and focus in on the key DFs. When these are presented to a group of managers, as most analysts will do in their development of DFs, someone invariably throws cold water on some of the suggested forces and suggests others. Our experience suggests that some of the most constructive debates occur when the DFs determination team tries to identify its relevant set of forces. Of course, it can often get even more interesting once this step is completed and their impacts are discussed.

The list below shows the completion of the first stage by a management group of a large, publicly funded university in South Africa.

Representative DFs in macro environment for a large public, South African university

Societal and demographic

- Increased diversity of students seeking university education.

- Question over the value of some credentials – particularly relative to experience.

- Increasing blurring of lines between trade, professional and traditional post-secondary education.

- Increasing desire by individuals for lifelong learning.

- Long-held concerns over social inequities and fragmentation, under-representation of black women.

- Increasing complexity of social problems.

- Continuing problems of getting enough 18–22 year olds into university in primary catchment regions.

- Changing views regarding the appropriate role of universities.

Economic

- Continued globalisation.

- Growth increasingly powered by entrepreneurship.

- Huge increases in participation rate of university students in China, India and Mexico.

- Onset of global recession.

- Unavailability of funding schemes or public funds to allow for access to quality university education.

- Impact of interest rates on student loans.

Political

- Ongoing blurring of post-secondary sector institutions such as colleges, technical institutes and universities.

- Uncertainties in direction of public support for universities.

- Declining public funding.

- Increasing governmental demand for accountability.

- Increased student activism due to higher tuition fees.

Technological

- Increasing demand for distance learning availability.

- Origination of new pedagogical platforms.

■ Expanded use of information technology in and out of the classroom.

■ Escalating rates of innovation.

■ Increasing value placed on knowledge.

This list illustrates a typical array of factors to emerge from this step. We recommend that you complete at least one other iteration to reduce these even further, prior to assessing their relative impact in Step 2. At the end of this step you should have a manageable list of DFs to consider. Our experience suggests that the list should have around five to ten forces to facilitate the next step of this analysis process.

Step 2: Assessing the impact of the DFs

Step 2 will require a more intense analytical effort than Step 1, because the DFs that remain on the list from Step 1 are all deemed to be important to some degree to the success of your industry and firm. All firms need to offer customers in their target markets products or services that meet their needs in a profitable manner, and the forces already identified impact all rivals in the industry. Now rank these DFs in order of their importance in driving the attractiveness of the industry, the level of profitability that may be achieved in the near future, and to provide a context in which strategy changes can be considered and thoughtful decisions made.

Your objective in this second step is to understand the external factors that will shape change in the industry and the difference these factors will make to it. Once the DFs have been identified from Step 1, you need to ask the following questions:

■ Are they valid?

■ How do we know?

■ How significant are each of them?

■ What is their strength?

■ Which ones can be altered?

■ Which ones cannot be altered?

■ Which ones can be altered quickly?

■ Which ones can only be altered slowly?

■ Which ones, if altered, would produce rapid change?

■ Which ones would only produce slow change?

■ What skills and/or information are needed and are available to change the forces?

■ Can you get the resources/capabilities needed to change them?

There are three common approaches applied at this point.

The first approach is to use a structured ranking approach. With a structured ranking approach, you need to consider all the DFs listed from Step 1 in pair-wise progression. In other words, take DF 1 and compare it with DF 2, and decide which is more important to the industry and the firm in the determination of strategy, making major decisions and setting of important policies. Next, compare DF 1 with the remaining DFs, then take DF 2 and compare it with the remaining DFs, and continue the process until all possible comparisons have been exhausted.

As you can quickly calculate, the number of pair-wise comparisons grows rapidly with the number of DFs. For six DFs, there are 15 comparisons; for eights DFs, there are 28 comparisons; and for ten DFs, there are 45 comparisons. You can readily see the advantages to taking care in selecting the initial DFs.

Our experience using this method is that some of the comparisons will be quickly accomplished, while others will bog down the group in discussion. It usually takes half a day to achieve consensus about the final list of DFs ranked in order of their impact. It is critical that you put in the appropriate effort at this point since it will enhance the quality of any complementary efforts that you subsequently perform, particularly in support of regularly conducted planning activities.

A second approach that many analysts take at this point is to assign a score to each force, from 1 (weak) to 7 (strong). The score is based on the strength of the force and the degree to which it is possible to influence this force. Next, calculate a total score for each force by adding across the two columns. An example of this is given in Table 5.1 for a player in the transportation manufacturing industry.

The third approach is to use a matrix that separates the forces on preselected dimensions. The following example uses 'importance' and 'uncertainty' to distinguish between the set of DFs. Importance rankings can be assigned to each of the DFs in the list using a scale of 1–4, with 1 being assigned to the DF of 'lowest importance' and 4 being assigned to the DF of 'highest importance'. The same process can be used for 'uncertainty', whereas 1 is assigned to DF with the 'lowest uncertainty' and 4 is assigned to the DF of 'highest uncertainty' in terms of their depth, direction impact. and evolution. Those with mean scores above 2.5 in the relevant range are rated 'high' in Figure 5.2, while those scoring below it are rated as 'low'.

Regardless of which of the three approaches are taken, another key facet of

Table 5.1 Ranking driving forces

Force	Strength	Ability to influence	Total (rank)
(i) Consumers seeking more specialised after-sale services	3	6	9 (5th)
(ii) Buyers want higher fuel economy	6	5	11 (2nd tie)
(iii) Better, safer, roads and highways allow for higher speeds	2	3	5 (7th)
(iv) Increased demands for passenger safety	4	4	8 (6th)
(v) New technologies allow more engine and fuel options	5	6	11 (2nd tie)
(vi) Demand for product is increasing most in China and India for the product	7	5	12 (1st)
(vii) Outsourcing options growing fast	4	6	10 (4th)

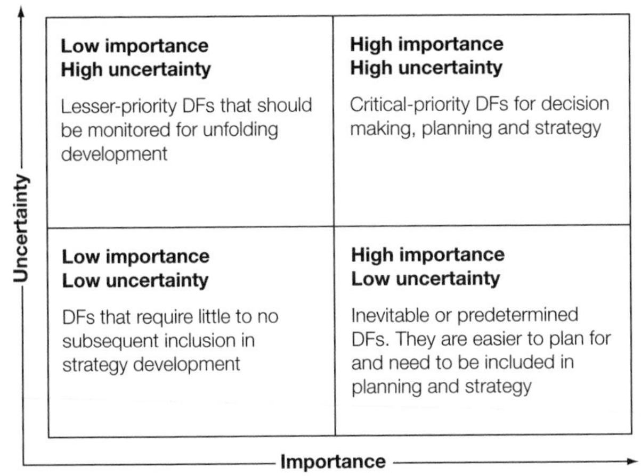

Low importance **High uncertainty** Lesser-priority DFs that should be monitored for unfolding development	**High importance** **High uncertainty** Critical-priority DFs for decision making, planning and strategy
Low importance **Low uncertainty** DFs that require little to no subsequent inclusion in strategy development	**High importance** **Low uncertainty** Inevitable or predetermined DFs. They are easier to plan for and need to be included in planning and strategy

Uncertainty (vertical axis) — *Importance* (horizontal axis)

Figure 5.2 Importance ranking of driving forces

this stage is to determine whether these DFs are acting to make the industry environment more or less attractive – as such, they should be combined with an industry analysis, possibly using Porter's Five Forces model[5] or something similar. The four questions related to the DF's impact on the industry environment that must be answered are as follows:

■ Are the DFs causing demand for the industry's product to increase or decrease?

■ Are the DFs making the bargaining power of other industry participants higher or lower?

■ Are the DFs acting to make competition more or less intense?

■ Will the DFs likely lead to higher or lower industry profitability?

The case study provides an illustration of DFA as it is applied to the digital music player industry. This relatively youthful industry is an interesting case study for DFA, because in 2009 it was still in a relatively early stage of its life cycle relative to the use of players for MP3 digital file formats, as well as being a spin-off of portable music players that used to play music formatted on CDs, which are in a mature stage of their life cycle.

Once you have performed these steps, your next task is to decide whether (strategic or tactical) actions taken to change the firm's strategy to address the driving force are feasible or not. If so, your goal is to devise a manageable course of action that does the following:

■ strengthens DFs with positive impacts on the industry and firm

■ weakens DFs with adverse impacts on the industry and firm

■ creates new positive DFs.

At this point, it is usually helpful for you to develop another set of tables, one for each of the DFs that has been identified as a priority. For each of these tables, outline in the first column the range of likely impacts that the DFs are expected to have on the industry. In the second column, begin identifying potential solutions that the firm may bring to bear in constructively addressing (that is, minimising the negative effects and maximising the positive effects) the impacts. The tables should look like Table 5.2.

The next step would require you to work through each of the proposed solutions. You would need to compare these options in terms of costs/benefits, risks/benefits, or via a pre-determined set of criteria used for assessing the relative attractiveness and value of the options. Comparing them against the current strategy of the firm is another key task to perform at this point, in order to gauge the degree of change required should the firm adopt the proposed solution, as well as the likelihood that the firm could implement it effectively; and, finally, analyse and identify the nature of competitor responses that the action may engender. DFs and competitive pressures do not affect all competitors in an industry in the same manner. Profit prospects vary from rival to rival based on the relative attractiveness of their market positions and their strategies in addressing the DFs.

Table 5.2 Impact and proposed solutions for driving force 1

Force 1: *Increasing environmental concerns* *Impact on industry*	*Proposed solutions*
Increasing demand for cars that can run on biofuels	■ Fund and support further research into alternative biofuels
	■ Develop new fuel delivery systems for cars
	■ Continue development on biofuel-burning engine materials
	■ Work with existing petrol suppliers and retailers to develop delivery infrastructure
Structural materials that can be recycled or will naturally break down at the end of their useful life	■ Fund and support further research into alternative materials; in particular, biodegradable ones
	■ Continue development of recycling collection capacities
	■ Work with local authorities to provide incentives to encourage recyclability
Greater fuel efficiency of vehicles	■ Continue development of hybrid engine technologies
	■ Provide more engines with partial cylinder managed shut-down capability
	■ Develop lighter materials to reduce weight
	■ Further develop computerised fuel-maximisation driving modules

The digital music industry

This case study provides an example of DFA as applied to the digital music player industry as at the end of 2008.

What are the major DFs affecting the digital music player industry? Are the forces indicating a more- or less-attractive industry environment from a profitability standpoint?

Growth levels of demand

You cannot go anywhere these days without seeing people walking around with tiny, increasingly colourful, boxed-shape listening devices (i.e. ear buds, ear phones) connected to their heads. Aside from being the most popularly given category of gifts ▶

during most of the last holiday-giving seasons globally, sales of MP3 and MP4 players have been soaring for years. Half of all music sold in the US is expected to be digital in 2011 and sales of downloaded music will surpass CD sales in 2012, according to a recent Forrester Research report titled 'The end of the music industry as we know it'. Digital music sales, the basic content input played on MP3 players, are expected to grow at a compound annual growth rate of 23 per cent over the next five years, reaching US$4.8 billion in revenue by 2012. As any scan of the technology news or consumer technology sites and the media will attest, both the digital music player market and the market for digital music are expected to continue experiencing a healthy growth. As technological advances spur the enhancement of the devices with more and more valuable features, sales both to new users as well as existing device owners will continue to remain robust.

Product innovation

Frequent product innovation is another characteristic of the industry. This product innovation is largely focused on new product designs, enhanced functionality, and aesthetics that make the products more portable, pleasant to look at (that is, some of these items are viewed as 'status symbols' when worn by their owners in some parts of the world) and easier to use. Firms continue to add useful features to MP3 and MP4 players such as telephone capability, touch screens, longer battery life, wireless file transfer, video-playing capacity, FM radio, appointment schedulers and calendars, contact databases, flash memory, voice capture and photographic capabilities. Many of the manufacturers are known for their product innovation capabilities, including Apple, Creative, Microsoft, Philips, Samsung and Sony, among others.

Format war and rights management

There are multiple formats of MP3 digital music files, as well as for MP4-playable video files, some of which can only be played on the format owner's own devices. Realnetworks offers its own formats, which also support Apple's basic format of choice, AAC, but does not support the extended proprietary version of AAC, which integrates an Apple-developed digital rights management system called *FairPlay*. Microsoft continues to promote its Windows Media Audio (WMA) standard that it would like to see emerge as the industry standard. Sony music players only worked with their proprietary software for many years. Fighting digital piracy and promoting fairness in using files, while making sure artists and music firms are properly compensated for their rights, remains at the heart of an ongoing global regulatory battle. Additionally, the recent entrance of major retail players such as Amazon has already driven the price of MP3 files down, adding pressure to Apple to lower its current prices for downloads.

Convergence

Coupled with product innovation, firms are increasingly working to make their MP3 or MP4 players and other personal electronics more versatile. For example, Apple developed the iPod Photo that allows users to transport and display photos; mobile phone makers, such as Sony and Nokia, are developing MP3 compatible sets; and personal digital assistant (PDA) makers, such as HP and PalmOne, have, or are developing, PDAs with phone, game, MP3 playing and digital photography capabilities. Most traditional home stereo manufacturers already offer stand-alone players that can play MP3 formats. Finally, MP3 playing capabilities are being increasingly included in new automotive stereo products, adding a different form of portability for playing music (at far higher speeds than while walking).

Growing use of the Internet

The increasing global adoption of broadband Internet service will help drive the market forward by increasing the source of supply and demand for the music to be played on the industry's devices. This also creates a need for a portable method for maintaining one's MP3 or video collections. This factor could especially benefit the manufacturers whose players are identified with popular subscription services. The ability to download a large amount of music or video in a relatively short time is a success factor for that segment of the MP3 and MP4 value chain. Growing use of the Internet will also lead to better informed and more MP4-amenable customers.

Changes in who uses the product and how it is used

An increasingly diverse, global customer base is using the industry's products in more varied ways. The industry's products are moving up the product life cycle from the early adopters to the mainstream; consequently, users are becoming less technologically sophisticated and more demanding on functionality, style and price. This also changes the nature of tactics and strategies that the major players in the industry will use in order to be successful, particularly around areas such as pricing, promotion, advertising, manufacturing and branding concerns.

The effect of DFs in this market can also be further analysed by answering the following four questions:

■ *What is the effect of the DFs on demand?* Virtually all of these changes should increase the level of demand for the industry's products. Increasing product innovation, especially in the area of convergence with PDA, wireless or telephone (e.g. smartphone) functionality, should lead to higher demand, especially from existing device owners. Growing use of the Internet and increasing broadband availability should also be a demand driver, as it increases the volume of content available, as well as the population of individuals who can potentially use the product.

■ *Are the DFs making the bargaining power of other industry participants higher or lower?* The resolution of the digital rights issue will clearly empower some players, whether it will be consumers who will have liberalised choice options for their digital music enjoyment, record firms or artists. Also, the eventual resolution of the format wars will also clearly empower some industry participants while neutralising the prospects of others. As such, there remains a high degree of uncertainty surrounding the resolution of this driving trend; however, it will have a significant impact on some firms, and industry participants will need to develop flexible strategies and contingency plans in case the trends go against their current strategy.

■ *Are the DFs increasing competition?* There is no doubt that the increased demand for, and increasing profitability of, products such as Apple's iPod will entice new and potentially powerful electronics manufacturers into the industry. The threat of new entrants is a key factor in the rivalry among sellers in the market. The high threat will cause the current players to compete against both each other and possible new entrants, specifically in the area of product innovation.

▶

■ *Will the DFs lead to higher profitability?* New entrants are expected to arise in the market, which will in turn increase supply. Demand will continue to be increased due to product innovations, market growth, and the increased evolution and advancement in Internet usage globally. It will be interesting to see whether demand or supply will be the stronger force in the coming years. It is reasonable to conclude that profitability will likely be based more on volume than margin in the future. This is a natural occurrence as a market matures. However, the rapid expansion of the market should help to limit the onset or duration of price wars from cutting margins to too great a degree. Because of these factors, the market should still be profitable, at least in the short term, especially for firms that can continue to efficiently add innovative features to their products that appeal to the more mainstream users.

6

Financial ratio and statement analysis

Description and purpose

A company's published annual report and accounts usually contain a bewildering array of figures, which are often difficult to analyse. *Financial statement analysis* provides managers with an understanding of a company's financial performance, competitive situation and future prospects. It also gives insight into the company's financial decision making and its operating performance. *Ratio analysis* provides insights into the relationships between two or more amounts in a company's financial statements.

Basic concepts underlying financial ratio and statement analysis (FRSA)

The basic equation that expresses the relationship of assets and claims on assets is called the accounting equation:

$$\text{Assets} = \text{Liabilities} + \text{Owners' equity}$$

Assets are generally classified into three categories:

- *Current assets.* Cash and other assets expected to be converted into cash within one year, such as marketable securities, accounts receivable, notes receivable, inventories and prepaid expenses.

- *Fixed assets.* Business assets that have relatively long lives and are used in the production or sale of goods and services, such as equipment, machinery, furniture and fixtures, land and plants.

- *Noncurrent assets.* Investments in securities and intangible assets such as patents, franchise costs and copyrights.

Liabilities are generally classified into two categories:

- *Current liabilities.* The amounts owed to creditors that are due within one year.

- *Long-term liabilities.* Claims of creditors that do not come due within one year, such as bonded indebtedness, long-term bank loans and mortgages.

Owners' equity is the claims of owners against the business. This is the residual amount computed by subtracting liabilities from assets. Its balance is increased by any profit and reduced by any losses incurred by the business.

Components of financial statements

Statements commonly used by analysts include the income statement, balance sheet, statement of changes in financial position and statement of changes in owners' equity.

- *The income statement* summarises the results of a company's operations in terms of revenue and expenses for a period of time called the accounting period. Net income is derived from the accrual measurement of revenue and expenses. The income statement is generally perceived as the most important financial statement because it reveals whether the shareholders' interests in the organisation have increased or decreased for the period after adjusting for dividends or other transactions with owners. The income statement also helps users to assess the amount, timing and uncertainty of future cash flows.

- *The balance sheet* shows what a company owns (its assets) and any claims against the company (liabilities and owners' equity) on a particular date. It provides a snapshot of a company's financial health at a particular point in time.

- *The position statement* (also known as the statement of changes in financial position) helps to explain how a company acquired and spent its money.

- *The statement of changes in owners' equity* shows the gap between the amount of owners' equity at the beginning and end of a period.

Applying ratio analysis to financial statements enables you to make judgements about the competitive success, failure and evolution of a company over time and to evaluate how it is performing compared with similar companies in the same industry. It can assist a company in gaining an awareness of competitors' strengths and weaknesses. For example, if you find weaknesses in a competitor's performance, then your company may be able to take measures to exploit them.

Assessing the appropriateness of ratios

There are three principal benchmarks used to assess the appropriateness of ratios.

The first benchmark is *the company's performance history*. It is useful to review the ratios in the current year relative to what they were over several previous years. This enables you to discover any favourable or unfavourable trends that are developing over time, as well as to identify any numbers that have changed dramatically in a defined period of time.

The second benchmark is *to compare a company with specific competitors*. If the competitors are publicly listed companies, obtain copies of their annual reports and compare each of the focal company's ratios with each of the competitor's. This is particularly helpful in identifying why the focal company is doing better or worse than specific competitors.

The third benchmark is *an industry-wide comparison*. You need to obtain data regarding industry averages, many of which can be accessed from Internet and government sources. Dun & Bradstreet and Robert Morris Associates are two examples of commercial sources that collect financial data, compute ratios by industry and publish the results. The information is often broken down by size of company and in a way that allows you to determine how far away from the norm any company is.

Strengths

FRSA is a helpful information overload tool. It can find patterns in large amounts of disconnected data through:

■ transforming financial data into manageable and meaningful outputs

■ connecting the dynamic income statement with the static balance sheet into one integrated analysis.

FRSA is versatile and easily amenable to internal company analysis and competitive analysis of rivals and industry structure. It allows you to determine a company's ability to succeed through its application of a generic strategy, such as low-cost producer, niche pursuer or differentiator. By combining the FRSA with numerous other techniques, such as those described in other chapters contained in this book, you can gain a good picture of a company's likelihood of strategic and competitive success.

Weaknesses

Financial ratios are based on historical accrual accounting information. As such, they do not offer the analyst any direct insights into cash flow, an important component of value-based management. This can be even more important with embryonic, entrepreneurial companies that have larger burn rates and cash needs during their earlier years.

Additionally a single ratio will not give you enough information to make a judgement about a company. Additional data are necessary to make these judgements.

Accountants do not include as assets certain items that are critical to the growth and well-being of a company in balance sheets, such as the quality of its employees. Financial statements virtually ignore these increasingly important intangible assets – a key source of competitive advantage in an information or knowledge-driven economy. FRSA is inherently limited as an analytical tool for companies with valuable brand names or corporate reputations, intellectually skilled workforces or other intellectual capital.

Not all financial statements are of equal quality. Reporting authorities and accounting overseers in separate countries may require different conventions, which can make comparisons difficult. Audited statements provide you with a higher probability of accurate financial information. However, published ratios are generally not subject to public audits, with the exception of the earnings per share (EPS) ratio.

Over-reliance on industry norms is akin to benchmarking for mediocrity instead of best practice. Even though it is important to use industry norms to evaluate financial performance against industry peers, caution should be applied in interpreting the results. Analysts who rely too much on industry comparisons risk leading their companies to the netherworld of what Michael Porter aptly describes as being 'stuck in the middle' of the industry's parabolic profit curve. To see how this can occur, consider an industry in which half of the rivals are pursuing a low-cost strategy while the other half are pursuing a differentiated strategy. Comparing a company's ratios to the industry norms will, by definition, target average performance. Success in meeting these average targets will necessarily relegate the company to the lowest point on the industry profit curve. At one end, the average company's cost structure will be higher than that of the low-cost specialists; at the other end, premium companies will surpass the average company's level of differentiation.

When using industry norms, you must also remain aware of comparing dissimilar industry groups – direct financial comparisons to rivals outside an industry group may only provide low short-term utility. Even comparisons within industry groups are fraught with difficulty when rival companies are operating on a different portion of the industry profit curve by virtue of their chosen low cost, differentiation or focus strategies. Additionally, because most industry norms are calculated from aggregated financial statements, rating a company's financial performance to a diversified company will cause a critical comparability problem if the lines of business are radically different.

Making internal comparisons to past company performance is also risky. One of several manifestations of this risk is complacency from seemingly adequate improvements, while in reality the company is slipping relative to the performance of rivals. This problem is especially prevalent in fast-growing markets where differences in relative competitive performance may not be painful in the short term but will nonetheless have serious repercussions on long-term competitive positioning.

You should also carefully consider the effects of management choices on the results of operations as reported in the financial statements. In closely held businesses, it is not uncommon for the financial statements to reflect the discretionary choices of the business owner or senior management. Sometimes significant adjustments can be required to restate the financial statements to accurately portray the operations of the business.

The choice of accounting method may have a significant impact on the income reported in the income statement and the value of the asset reported in the balance sheet. This is especially pertinent when doing international competitor comparisons and when competitors have multinational operations that potentially utilise different accounting schemes. Other technical considerations that could distort the validity of the comparison include differences in accounting policies (different depreciation schedules, inventory valuation and capitalisation), account classification or year-ends across companies.

Even when a company's financial ratios appear to conform to industry averages, this does not mean that the company has no financial or other strategic management problems. For example, the company may be neglecting to exploit a clear differentiation advantage through which it could outstrip average industry performance. Alternatively, perhaps the company's finances look good at the moment, but a serious competitive threat could reverse them in the near future.

In short, financial ratio analysis is a useful tool for analysing the decisions of management as they are manifest in the marketplace, but it cannot replace the insights afforded by the application of a variety of analysis tools.

How to do it

Performing an FSRA can be divided into several steps:

1 Choose the appropriate ratios to analyse.

2 The appropriate sources must be located to provide the raw data in which to calculate the ratios – this is a topic better covered by books on the larger competitive intelligence data collection process.

3 Calculate the ratios and make comparisons of the ratios.

4 A check is performed for opportunities and problems.

Following are some common ratios for analysing financial statements.

Table 6.1 shows the necessary formulas to use.

Activity or efficiency ratios

These include inventory, accounts receivable, and fixed and total asset turnover ratios.

Inventory

Depending on the nature of the business (retail, wholesale, service or manufacturing), the efficiency of inventory management may have a significant impact on cash flow and, ultimately, its success or failure.

■ *Average inventory investment period*

$$\frac{\text{Average inventory}}{\text{investment period}} = \frac{\text{current inventory balance}}{\text{average daily costs of goods sold (COGS)}}$$

This measures the amount of time it takes to convert £1 of cash outflow used to purchase inventory to £1 of sales or accounts receivable from the sale of the inventory.

The average investment period for inventory is similar to the average collection period for accounts receivable. A longer average inventory investment period requires a higher investment in inventory. A higher investment in inventory means less cash is available for other cash outflows, such as paying bills.

■ *Inventory to sales ratio*

$$\text{Inventory to sales ratio} = \frac{\text{inventory}}{\text{sales for the month}}$$

This looks at the company's investment in inventory in relation to its monthly sales. It helps identify recent increases in inventory and is a quick and easy way of looking at recent changes in inventory levels because it uses monthly sales and inventory information.

This ratio will help predict early cash flow problems related to a business's inventory.

However, where the only information available is based on inventory information from the previous year, it can be used to provide a rough guide.

■ *Inventory turnover analysis*

$$\text{Inventory turnover} = \frac{\text{sales}}{\text{inventory of finished goods month}}$$

This is the most basic tool for assessing the organisation's investment in inventory. It helps you to decide if the company's investment in an inventory item or groups of items is excessive, too low or just right. From a cash flow perspective, performing turnover analysis is particularly useful for finding inventory items that are overstocked.

Accounts receivable

Accounts receivable represent sales for which payment has not yet been collected. If the business normally extends credit to its customers, the payment of accounts receivable is likely to be its single most important source of cash inflows.

The following analysis tools can be used to help determine the effect the company's accounts receivable are having on its cash flow:

■ *Average collection period*

$$\text{Average collection period} = \frac{\text{current accounts receivable balance}}{\text{average daily sales (average daily sales} = \text{annual sales/365)}}$$

This measures the length of time it takes to convert average sales into cash. This measurement defines the relationship between accounts receivable and cash flow. A longer average collection period requires a higher investment in accounts receivable. A higher investment in accounts receivable means less cash is available to cover cash outflow.

■ *Accounts receivable to sales ratio*

$$\text{Accounts receivable to sales ratio} = \frac{\text{accounts receivable}}{\text{sales}}$$

This looks at the company's investment in accounts receivable in relation to sales. It helps you to identify recent increases in accounts receivable and can serve as a quick and easy way to examine any recent changes. The more recent information of the accounts receivable to sales ratio will quickly point out cash flow problems related to the business's accounts receivable.

■ *Accounts receivable turnover*

$$\text{Accounts receivable turnover} = \frac{\text{accounts receivable}}{\text{average daily sales}}$$

This is a measure of the average length of time it takes a company to collect the sales made on credit.

Asset turnover

This is the ratio of sales (on the income statement) to the value of the company's assets (on its balance sheet):

$$\text{Asset turnover} = \frac{\text{revenue}}{\text{assets}}$$

Asset turnover indicates how well a business is using its assets to generate sales. Generally, the higher the ratio the better because a high ratio indicates that the business has less money tied up in assets for each pound of sales revenue. A declining ratio may indicate that it has over-invested in plant, equipment or other fixed assets. Companies with low profit margins tend to have high asset turnover; those with high profit margins have lower asset turnover – this indicates their pricing strategy. In computing this ratio, it may be helpful to compute total assets by averaging the total assets at the beginning and end of the accounting period.

This ratio indicates how well a company is using all of its business assets to generate revenue, rather than just its inventories or fixed assets. A high asset turnover ratio means a higher return on assets, which can compensate for a low profit margin.

Leverage or solvency analysis ratios

Commonly used solvency ratios are debt to equity, debt to assets, coverage of fixed costs and interest coverage.

This group of ratios is designed to help you assess the degree of financial risk that a business faces. Financial risk, in this context, means the extent to which the company has debt obligations that must be met, regardless of its cash flow. By looking at these ratios, the analyst can decide whether the company's level of debt is appropriate or not.

■ *Debt to equity*

$$\text{Debt to equity} = \frac{\text{total debt}}{\text{total shareholders' equity}}$$

This indicates the degree of financial leverage that the company is using to enhance its return. It provides a measure of the funds provided by creditors versus the funds provided by owners.

A rising debt to equity ratio may signal that further increases in debt caused by purchases of inventory or fixed assets should be curtailed.

Improving this ratio involves either paying off debt or increasing the amount of earnings retained in the business until after the balance sheet date.

■ *Debt to assets*

$$\text{Debt to assets} = \frac{\text{total debt}}{\text{total assets}}$$

This compares the percentage of assets financed by creditors to the percentage financed by the business owners. Historically, a debt to asset ratio of no more than 50 per cent has been considered prudent. A higher ratio indicates a possible overuse of leverage, and it may indicate potential problems in meeting the debt payments.

Improving this ratio means taking steps either to increase the value of the company's assets or to pay off debt. If it goes down the route of paying off debt, it will also improve its current ratio and debt to equity ratio.

■ *Fixed charge coverage*

$$\frac{\text{Fixed charge}}{\text{coverage}} = \frac{\text{profits before taxes and interest} + \text{lease obligations}}{\text{total interest charges} + \text{lease obligations}}$$

This shows the company's ability to meet its fixed obligations of all types – the higher the number, the better.

Obviously, a company's inability to meet any fixed obligation is a threat to its well-being. Many working capital loan agreements will specify that a company must maintain this ratio at a specified level so that the lender has some assurance that the company will continue to be able to make its payments.

■ *Interest coverage*

$$\text{Interest coverage ratio} = \frac{\text{operating income}}{\text{interest expense}}$$

This is also known as the times interest earned ratio. It is similar to the times fixed charges earned ratio but focuses more narrowly on the interest portion of the company's debt payments.

By comparing the ratio of operating income to interest expense, you can measure how many times the company's interest obligations are covered by earnings from its operations. The higher the ratio, the bigger the company's cushion and the more able it is to meet interest payments. If this ratio declines over time, it's an indication that the company's financial risk is increasing.

Liquidity analysis ratios

These ratios indicate the ease of turning assets into cash. They include the current ratio and quick ratio. Liquidity ratios are sometimes called working capital ratios (the difference between current assets and current liabilities). Generally, the higher they are, the better, especially if the company is relying to any significant extent on creditor money to finance its assets.

■ *Current ratio*

$$\text{Current ratio} = \frac{\text{total current assets}}{\text{total current liabilities}}$$

This is one of the most popular measures of financial strength. It is a good indicator of a company's ability to pay its short-term obligations.

The main question this ratio addresses is: 'Does the company have enough current assets to meet the payment schedule of its current debts with a margin of safety for possible losses in current assets, such as inventory shrinkage or collectable accounts?' The higher the ratio, the more liquidity the company has. A generally acceptable rule of thumb for a current ratio is 2:1. But whether a specific ratio is satisfactory depends on the nature of the business and the characteristics of its current assets and liabilities. The minimum acceptable current ratio is 1:1, but that relationship is usually suggestive of potential risks or problems.

■ *Quick ratio*

$$\text{Quick ratio} = \frac{\text{cash} + \text{government securities} + \text{receivables} - \text{inventory}}{\text{total current liabilities}}$$

This is also known as the acid test ratio and is one of the best measures of liquidity. It describes how quickly a company can turn its current assets into cash.

The quick ratio is a more exacting measure than the current ratio. By excluding inventories, it concentrates on highly liquid assets with values that are fairly certain. It helps answer the question: 'If all sales revenues stop, could the business meet its current obligations with the readily convertible "quick" funds on hand?'

An acid test of 1:1 is considered satisfactory unless the majority of a company's 'quick assets' are in accounts receivable, and the pattern of accounts receivable collection lags behind the schedule for paying current liabilities.

■ *Working capital*

$$\text{Working capital} = \text{current assets} - \text{current liabilities}$$

This is the amount of liquid assets a company has to build its business, fund its growth and produce shareholder value.

The best way to look at current assets and current liabilities is to combine them into 'working capital'. Working capital can be positive or negative. If a company has ample positive working capital, it has the cash on hand to pay for the items it needs. If it has negative working capital, its current liabilities are greater than its current assets, and it has less ability to pay for the items it needs. A competitor with positive working capital will always outperform a company with negative working capital.

Profitability analysis ratios

These ratios are probably the most important indicators of a business's financial success – they demonstrate the performance and growth potential of the business. The most common of these include return on assets, return on equity, profit margin (which can be in either gross or net form) and asset turnover.

■ *Return on assets*

$$\text{Return on assets (ROA)} = \frac{\text{net income}}{\text{total assets}}$$

This is the ratio of net income to total assets. It is a measure of how well a business is using its assets to produce more income. It can be viewed as a combination of two other ratios: net profit margin (ratio of net income to sales) and asset turnover (ratio of sales to total assets). A high return on assets can be attributed to a high profit margin, a rapid turnover of assets, or a combination of both.

■ *Return on investment (ROI)/return on equity*

$$\text{Return on equity (ROE)} = \frac{\text{net income}}{\text{total shareholders' equity}}$$

This is the ratio of net income (from the income statement) to net worth or shareholders' equity (from the balance sheet). It shows what the company earned on its investment in the business during the accounting period. This ratio compares a business's return on equity to what it might have earned on the stock market during the same accounting period. Over time, a business should be generating at least the same return that it could earn in more passive investments, such as government bonds. A high return on equity may be a result of a high return on assets, extensive use of debt financing, or a combination of the two.

In analysing both ROE and ROA, don't forget to consider the effects of inflation on the book value of the assets. While financial statements show all assets at their book value (original cost minus depreciation), the replacement value of many older assets may be substantially higher. A business with older assets would generally show higher return percentages than a business with newer assets.

■ *Gross profit margin*

$$\text{Gross profit margin} = \frac{\text{gross profits}}{\text{sales}}$$

This is the amount of sales pounds remaining after the COGS has been deducted. If a company's gross profit margin is declining over time, it may mean that its inventory management needs to be improved, or that its selling prices are not rising as fast as the costs of the goods it sells. If the company is a manufacturer, it could mean that its costs of production are rising faster than its prices, and adjustments on either side (or both) may be necessary.

The net profit margin shows the company's bottom line: how much of each sales pound is ultimately available for the owners to draw out of the business or to receive as dividends. This ratio takes into account all of the company's expenses, including income taxes and interest.

You should have some idea of the prospective range of the company's profit margin, which will in large part be determined from historical data. If a company fails to meet its targets, it could mean that it has set unrealistic goals or is not managing as efficiently and effectively as it could. However, the ratio itself will not point to what a company might be doing wrong – looking at the gross margin or operating margin is a better way to address that problem.

The absolute level of profit may provide an indication of the size of the business, but on its own it says very little about company performance. To evaluate the level of profit, profit must be compared and related to other aspects of the business. Profit must also be compared with the amount of capital invested in the business and to sales revenue.

Profitability ratios will inevitably reflect the business environment of the time, so the business, political and economic climate must also be considered when looking at the trend of profitability for one company over time. Comparisons with other businesses in the same industry can give an indication of how well management is performing compared with other companies in the same business environment.

Other analysis ratios – capital market or shareholder returns

The use of capital market or shareholder returns analysis ratios is probably more important for investors than it is for strategic or competitive analysis. These are more commonly thought of as investment measures as opposed to performance measures.

■ *Earnings per share*

$$\text{Earnings per share (EPS)} = \frac{\text{net income} - \text{dividends on preferred stock}}{\text{average outstanding shares}}$$

This indicates the profitability of a company. Company earnings are income from sales or investment after paying expenses. The way in which a business conducts its operations is important when evaluating a company's earnings. Companies that are devoting significant resources to creating a new product may have relatively low earnings, but that can change when sales of the new product grow and profits rise. Meanwhile, companies that have strong earnings but are not investing adequate funds into the business may have significant problems in the future.

■ *Price/earnings ratio*

$$\text{Price/earnings (P/E) ratio} = \frac{\text{current market value per share}}{\text{EPS}}$$

This is often referred to as 'the Multiple'. The earnings per share figure is usually from the last four quarters (the trailing P/E ratio), but sometimes it is from the estimates of the earnings expected over the next four quarters (the projected P/E ratio) or from the sum of the last two quarters and the estimates of the next two quarters.

For the most part, a high P/E means high projected earnings in the future. A P/E ratio on its own doesn't give much information; however, it is useful to compare the P/E ratios of other companies in the same industry to the market in general or against the company's own historical P/E ratios.

Table 6.1 Financial ratios

Activity or efficiency ratios

Average inventory investment period
Average inventory investment period = current inventory balance/average daily COGS

(The average daily cost of goods sold (COGS) is computed by dividing your annual COGS by 365 days.)

Inventory to sales
Inventory to sales ratio = inventory/sales for the month

Inventory turnover analysis
Inventory turnover = sales/inventory of finished goods

Accounts receivable ratios

Average collection period
Average collection period = current accounts receivable balance/average daily sales

(average daily sales = annual sales/365)

Accounts receivable to sales
Accounts receivable to sales ratio = accounts receivable/sales

Accounts receivable turnover
Accounts receivable turnover = accounts receivable/average daily sales

Asset turnover
Asset turnover = revenue/assets

Leverage or solvency analysis ratios

Debt to equity
Debt to equity = total debt/total shareholders' equity

Debt to assets
Debt to assets = total debt/total assets

Fixed charge coverage
$$\text{Fixed charge coverage} = \frac{\text{profits before taxes and interest} + \text{lease obligations}}{\text{total interest charges} + \text{lease obligations}}$$

Interest coverage
Interest coverage ratio = operating income/interest expense

Liquidity analysis ratios

Current ratio
Current ratio = total current assets/total current liabilities

Quick ratio
$$\text{Quick ratio} = \frac{\text{cash} + \text{government securities} + \text{receivables} - \text{inventory}}{\text{total current liabilities}}$$

Liquidity analysis ratios

Working capital
Working capital = current assets − current liabilities

Profitability analysis ratios

Return on assets
Return on assets (ROA) = net income/total assets

Return on investment (ROI)/return on equity
Return on equity (ROE) = net income/total shareholders' equity

Gross profit margin
Gross profit margin = gross profits/sales

Other analysis ratios – capital market or shareholder returns

Earnings per share

Earnings per share (EPS) = $\dfrac{\text{Net income} - \text{dividends on preferred stock}}{\text{Average outstanding shares}}$

Price/earnings ratio

Price/earnings (P/E) ratio = current market value per share/EPS

Methods of ratio or measure comparison

No single ratio has a meaning by itself, but comparing ratios is critical for effective financial ratio analysis. A helpful solution to combat analytical myopia is to strike a balance between the industry norm, historical analysis/internal benchmarking and competitive external benchmarking approaches.

There are two basic ways of using financial ratios. The first way is to compare the company's ratios with those of other companies in the industry. The second way is to compare the company's present ratios with its own past performance ratios.

Industrial comparison

In industrial comparison we look at the company's performance in relationship to its competitors to show any differences in their operating efficiency. Once the problem is found, the company can take action to correct it. These industry averages can be found in publications like Dun & Bradstreet's Key Business Ratios.

There are several ways of obtaining financial ratios or comparisons for industries and companies, some of which are free and others that are available for a fee, as described in Table 6.2.

Table 6.2 Information sources for financial statement analysis

Resource	Free/for fee
Yahoo! Finance UK provides users with information on a large selection of public companies listed in the UK, including contact information, business summaries, officer and employee information, sector and industry classifications, business and earnings announcement summaries, and financial statistics and ratios. Yahoo adds stock charts based on historical data from Commodity Systems, Inc. (CSI), and links to other resources. Links to other Finance Yahoos across the world are listed towards the bottom of the page.	Free

Available from http://uk.finance.yahoo.com

Google Finance provides information on public and private companies   Free
including market data, interactive charts, ratios, news, company
management, financial results and key competitors. It also provides links
to other sources, including blogs. Stock prices are from the UK but some
information is available from stock exchanges outside the UK.

Available from http://www.google.co.uk/finance

Thomson Reuters, a global information company, has extensive   Free/for a fee
investment information available on equities. In addition to financials,
news, ratios, stock price charts, it also provides links to research reports
(some free), and sector and industry ratios. Importantly, it provides free
information on public companies listed around the world.

Available from http://www.reuters.com/finance

The **UK Companies Office** Webcheck Service provides access to   Free/for a fee
financial statements for listed UK companies. However, it is only
available from Monday to Saturday 7.00–12 midnight UK time. It has
invaluable links to companies' offices around the world, many of which
are free.

Available from http://www.companiesoffice.co.uk

Corporate Information provides extensive research reports on   Free
approximately 31,000 publicly traded companies in over 55 countries.
Up to ten years of sales, earnings and price history, some of which is
free of charge. There are also free top 100 lists of companies ranked by
market capitalisation, sales, operating profit margin, 52-week price
change and three-year sales growth.

Available from www.corporateinformation.com

Financial Times – basic background information and selected key   For a fee
financials for quoted companies.

Available from www.ft.com

LexisNexis – financial information on companies world-wide from a   For a fee
variety of sources and publishers.

Available from www.lexisnexis.com

D&B–Duns Financial Records Plus® (DFR) provides up to three years   For a fee
of comprehensive financial statements for over 2.9 million private
and public companies. Depending on the company, information provided
may include balance sheet, income statement, and 14 of the most
widely used business ratios for measuring solvency, efficiency and profitability.

Available from http://www.dialog.com

Key Business Ratios on the Web is an online analysis tool that   For a fee
provides immediate access to competitive benchmarking data that are
updated twice a year. Obtain industry benchmarks compiled from D&B's
database of public and private companies, choosing from 14 key
business ratios (choose a one-year or three-year set of ratios) for over
800 lines of business.

Available from http://kbr.dnb.com/login/KBRHome.asp/

Resource	*Free/for fee*
Almanac of Business and Industrial Financial Ratios is a comprehensive resource that puts 50 comparative performance indicators at a practitioner's command and covers all of North America (US, Canada and Mexico) using NAICS data. The *Almanac* provides financial information that is calculated and derived from the latest available IRS data on nearly 5 million US, and international companies. It provides performance data for 50 operating and financial factors in 199 industries.	For a fee
Available from http://www.amazon.com/Almanac-Business-Industrial-Financial-Ratios/dp/0808017594	
The Value Line Investment Survey is a comprehensive source of information and advice on approximately 1,700 stocks, more than 90 industries, the stock market and the economy.	For a fee
Available from www.valueline.com	
Standard & Poor's Industry Surveys are the fastest way to come up to speed on the players and events impacting over 50 of the largest North American and global industries. Each report is authored by a Standard & Poor's industry research analyst and includes the following sections: Current Environment, Industry Trends, How the Industry Operates, Key Industry Ratios and Statistics, How to Analyse a Company, Glossary of Industry Terms, Additional Industry Information References and Comparative Company Financial Analysis.	For a fee
Available from http://sandp.ecnext.com/coms2/page_industry	
Worldscope Fundamentals is an extensive source of financial data available from Thomson (formerly Datastream) including Financial Ratios (annual and five-year averages) including: growth rates, profitability, leverage, liquidity, asset utilisation, foreign business statistics, loan losses and deposits (for banks), earning assets (for insurance companies), footnotes to financial ratios.	For a fee
Available from http://www.thomsonreuters.com/products_services/financial/worldscope_fundamentals	
Moody's Global Credit Research service contains ratings and in-depth research on over 6,000 corporate, municipal and structured finance issuers in over 100 countries. Issuer ratings and rating methodologies are free. Corporate Financial Metrics (FM) enable clients to access the models, standard reports and rating methodologies used by Moody's analysts in the rating process.	Free/for a fee
Available from http://moodysfm.moodys.com/	
Factiva Companies & Executives™ provides competitor analysis, financial statements and regulatory filings, targeted news, executive biographies and more. The information that covers companies, industries and executives, is sourced from the most respected financial publishers including D&B, Reuters Fundamentals, Standard & Poor's, Dow Jones, with *The Wall Street Journal* and more than 10,000 authoritative news publications and databases.	

Available from http://www.factiva.com/products/fce/fce.asp?node=menuElem1822

Bureau van Dijk Electronic Publishing – The full BvDEP collection of priced services covers information on approaching 60 million companies around the globe. BvDEP's products include ORBIS, AMADEUS, FAME, BANKSCOPE and the MINT range of products designed for end users. They also produce the mergers and acquisitions database ZEPHYR. There is a free company search function on their MINT portal – www.mintbusinessinfo.com   Free/for a fee

Available from www.bvdep.com

OneSource pulls together company information from a variety of sources world-wide. Information Partners include Worldscope, Graham & Whiteside, Dun & Bradstreet, Jordans and Investext. Market research, general and industry news are also available.   For a fee

Available from www.onesource.com

Skyminder provides credit and financial information on companies world-wide from a variety of sources.   For a fee

Available from www.skyminder.com

For additional information on possible in-country sources around the world of financial information have a look at RBA (Rhodes-Blakeman Associates). The links they provide in their business resources section will take you to a wonderful array of business information sites on the Internet.

Available from http://www.rba.co.uk/sources/finars.htm

Trade associations and individual companies often compute ratios for their industries and make them available to analysts. Published financial statements on the Internet also offer a source of raw material for companies not covered by these sources.

To deal with corporations of significantly different sizes in a particular industry, it can be helpful to create 'common-size financial statements'. The common size is usually 100. This procedure can help you to identify when a competitor departs from industry norms. It will allow you to ask a more refined set of questions in order to gain an understanding of the causes driving this phenomenon.

Across time performance

You can also spot problems by comparing a company's present performance to how well it did over the past few years. This will give an indication of how well they are progressing in correcting any problems. By looking at the past trend, a company can determine how effective it is in accomplishing its goals. You should use the same time frame in making any comparison. If you don't, effects caused by recessions or seasonal fluctuations could result in erroneous conclusions or judgements.

Consolidation and segmented analysis

Financial statements of public companies are legally mandated to provide segmented reporting in addition to consolidated operations. Most countries require public companies to provide enough information to explain about three quarters of the company's revenue. However, due to the competitive sensitivity of segmented information, public companies generally follow the letter of the law rather than the spirit of the law; that is, proprietary concerns outweigh the need for public accessibility to information. Therefore, segmented reporting only includes the bare minimum of information regarding the revenue, net income and total assets of each segment. The only supplement to this meagre reporting is information about the industry and the geographic dispersion of its facilities and customers.

Although segmented reporting is certainly more valuable than consolidated information when comparing a company to its distinctly diversified rivals, it should not be relied upon. The accuracy and comparability will be minimal because segmented revenue will be derived from internal transfer prices, and the basis for allocating costs will be unknown to the external analyst.

Despite the requirement to reconcile or integrate the segment information back into the consolidated statements, segmented data will not provide enough information to calculate many ratios. Further, even when ratios can be calculated, you must remain aware of these limitations when performing ratio analysis on segmented data.

Remember that a company's financial statements are only a starting point for analysis. If a statement shows that accounts receivable have experienced a significant downward trend over the last few years, it could mean that the company is collecting the accounts more aggressively (which is good), or it could possibly mean that it is writing off accounts as uncollectable too soon (which is bad). Individual numbers aren't good or bad in themselves. You may have to dig behind any numbers for the reason. The key is to use FRSA to spot trends and anomalies, and then follow these up with further investigation.

To complete the picture, you must acquire more information about the company's products, people, technology and other resources that may give it a competitive advantage in the marketplace. One of the best sources of supplemental information is the nonfinancial section of the annual report. This section often provides an outline of top management's views on the company's future and ability to compete.

FRSA is a critical part of a larger, integrated financial statement analysis plan. This plan should include the following key steps:

1 Determine the objectives of the financial statement analysis.

2 Review the current and predicted economic conditions in the industry in which the company operates.

3 Consult the annual report and other regulatory filings to glean information about management and the company's accounting methods.

4 Analyse the financial statements using the means described in this chapter.

5 Draw relevant conclusions based on the initial objectives.

Dell Inc. in 2005

In seeking to assess Dell's financial performance during the period 1998–2004, the company's financial statements needed to be assessed. Financial ratios indicate the following:

▪ Dell's revenue grew at a compound annual rate of 22.4 per cent from fiscal 1998 to fiscal 2004.

▪ Earnings rose from $944 million in fiscal 1998 to $2,645 million in fiscal 2004 – a compound average growth rate (CAGR) of 18.7 per cent.

▪ Diluted earnings per share rose from $0.32 in 1998 to $1.01 per share in fiscal 2004 – a CAGR of 21.1 per cent.

▪ The company earned 42.1 per cent return on shareholders' equity in fiscal 2004 versus 43.5 per cent in fiscal 2003, 26.5 per cent in fiscal 2002, 38.7 per cent in 2001, 31.3 per cent in 2000, 62.9 per cent in 1999 and 73.0 per cent in 1998.

▪ The number of outstanding shares displayed a downward trend.

▪ Profit margins were good and have improved since 2002 but were still not as high as the period 1998–1999:

	2004	2003	2002	2001	2000	1999	1998
Gross profit margin	18.2%	17.9%	17.7%	20.8%	20.7%	22.5%	22.1%
Operating profit margin	8.6	8.0	5.7	8.4	9.0	11.2	10.7
Net profit margin	6.4	6.0	4.0	6.8	6.6	8.0	7.7

▪ Fiscal 2002 was not a good year for Dell.

▪ Operating expenses as a percentage of sales revenue were showing a downward trend – a clear sign of improving efficiency:

▶

1998	1999	2000	2001	2002	2003	2004
11.4%	11.3%	11.7%	11.9%	11.7%	9.9%	9.7%

- The company's R&D spending increased from $204 million in 1998 to $464 million in fiscal 2004 – but was down from 1.65% of revenues in 1998 to 1.11% in 2004 (is this a sign of growing R&D efficiency, a weaker management commitment to R&D or a lesser need for Dell to perform R&D?).

- The company's operations were generating positive cash flows – $3.5 billion in fiscal 2003 and $3.7 billion in fiscal 2004.

- The company was in a strong cash position, with $11.9 billion in cash and marketable securities as of 30 January 2004.

- The company had little long-term debt – $505 million in 2004 versus shareholders' equity of $6.3 billion, a very good debt-to-equity ratio.

As a result of financial ratio and statement analysis, it is fair to say that Dell's financial performance has been reasonably impressive (aside from fiscal 2002) and that the company is in good overall financial shape – declining expense percentages, low long-term debt, $11.9 billion in cash and short-term investments, and improving profit margins since the lows of 2002.

Source: Data adapted from 'Dell Inc. in 2005: A winning strategy?', Case Study 7 in Thompson, A.A., Gamble, J.E. and Strickland, A.J., *Strategy: Winning in the Marketplace*, 2nd edn (New York: McGraw-Hill/Irwin, 2006).

7

Five Forces Industry Analysis

Description and purpose

The Five Forces Industry Analysis, developed by Michael Porter,[1] is designed to give you an understanding of an industry and its participants. The purpose of industry analysis is to analyse the economic and market forces that will ultimately influence an industry's profit potential. Identifying the profit potential or 'attractiveness' of an industry provides the foundation for bridging the gap between your firm's external environment and its internal resources.

Porter classifies the five forces or 'rules of industry competition' as follows:

1 Threat of new entrants.

2 Bargaining power of suppliers.

3 Bargaining power of buyers.

4 Threat of substitute products or services.

5 Degree of rivalry among existing competitors.

The objective of this analysis is to:

- identify the profit potential of an industry
- identify the forces that would harm your company's profitability in that industry
- protect and extend your competitive advantage
- anticipate changes in industry structure.

A proper understanding of the five forces is important in developing your company's competitive strategy. The ultimate aim of the analysis is in developing competitive actions to cope with and, ideally, influence or change these forces in favour of your firm.

The scope of each of the five forces is covered in the following sections.

Threat of new entrants

Everything else being equal, industries that are very easy for new organisations to enter are more difficult to compete in than ones with higher barriers. The nature of entry barriers affects the level of difficulty facing companies wishing to enter an industry. If entry barriers are low, new entrants will increase the demand and prices for inputs, resulting in lower industry profitability. New entrants ordinarily face several entry barriers. These include things such as:

- *Entry-deterring price.* The cost of entry exceeds forecasted revenue – often, existing players will lower their prices to thwart a competitive entry.

- *Incumbent retaliation.* Existing companies often have substantial resources and the willpower to fight new entrants.

- *High entry costs.* Often, substantial portions of the start-up costs are unrecoverable.

- *Experience effects.* The accumulated experience of existing companies in the industry often translates into lower cost structures.

- *Other cost advantages.* Access to valuable inputs and suppliers, proprietary technology or the best locations may already be controlled by existing companies.

- *Product differentiation.* The high cost of marketing new brands may pose significant entry barriers not faced by existing companies that have well-known brands, customer loyalty and the flexibility to co-brand other products.

- *Distribution access.* This also includes the need to pay incentives to distributors to persuade them to carry new products.

- *Government.* Public bodies can provide subsidies for existing companies, enforce compliance with regulations or develop policies that restrict entry.

- *Switching costs.* It can be expensive or inconvenient for customers to switch to a new product.

Bargaining power of suppliers

Suppliers may have the ability to influence the cost, availability and quality of input resources to companies in the industry. When considering this force, suppliers must be thought of more broadly than just those providing raw material inputs. This group can also include those groups governing or providing labour (trade unions or professional bodies, for example), locations (landing slots at airports) or channels (the broadcasting spectrum), among other things.

Suppliers' bargaining power may be influenced by the following:

- *Concentration.* Supplier bargaining power will be high where an industry is dominated by fewer players than the industry it sells to unless substitute inputs are available.

- *Diversification.* The proportion of total sales that a supplier has with a particular industry will vary inversely with supplier power. For example, if a supplier's revenue is totally sourced from one industry, its power over the industry will be lower than a supplier that only sells 20 per cent of its total goods to an industry.

- *Switching costs.* Supplier bargaining power will be weaker if companies in an industry can switch suppliers easily or inexpensively.

- *Organisation.* Supplier organisations industry associations/groups or trade unions or the presence of patents or copyright will increase supplier power, and thus their collective bargaining power.

- *Government.* In many economies, the government can function as a supplier, whether of land, rights to compete, licences, and so on, and can therefore exert substantial bargaining power.

Bargaining power of buyers

Buyers can influence industry structure and force prices down by such actions as comparison shopping or by raising quality expectations.

Buyers' bargaining power may be influenced by the following:

- *Differentiation.* Products with unique attributes will decrease buyers' power. Commodity products that are difficult to distinguish will increase their power.

- *Concentration.* Where there are few buyers and they represent a high proportion of a company's sales (for example, a government body that serves as the primary buyer of pharmaceuticals for citizens living within its boundary), buyer power will be high.

- *Profitability*. Buyers with low margins, lesser resources or lower profits will be more price-sensitive.

- *Quality*. Where quality is important, buyers may be less price-sensitive.

Threat of substitute products or services

Not only does an organisation have to worry about competition from companies within the industry seeking to provide similar products or services to a group of customers, it also needs to concern itself with companies from outside the existing industry which seek to provide alternatives not provided by companies in the existing industry. Industry competitors would always prefer the threat of substitute products or services to be low. Market displacement by existing or potential substitutes can be influenced by the following:

- *Relative price/performance trade-off*. The risk of substitutes is high where existing products or services offer favourable attributes at low cost.

- *Switching costs*. The threat of substitution is low where switching costs – from one product or service that customers are currently using – are high.

- *Profitability*. A reliable substitute product that is profitable may displace or disrupt existing products.

Degree of rivalry among existing players

Of all the five forces, rivalry among existing players is nearly always the most important in determining the attractiveness and potential profitability of an industry. All else being equal, existing companies in an industry prefer to face lesser competitive intensity and rivalry. Strangely enough, and for a variety of sometimes counter-intuitive reasons, some degree of rivalry and a small number of competitors are typically superior to no rivalry or what is otherwise known as a monopoly situation. The intensity of competition within an industry is determined by the following:

- *Market growth*. When strong, market growth in the existing industry reduces rivalry and thereby the probability of retaliation.

- *Cost structure*. When fixed costs are high, over-capacity occurs during demand troughs, and the fight for market share by existing rivals intensifies.

- *Barriers to exit*. For low-profit companies, barriers to exit include asset specialisation, fixed costs of exit, emotional attachment or the product's market importance in a company's overall strategic intentions. The higher these are, the more intense the rivalry will be in an industry.

■ *Product switching.* Product differentiation may protect the company from unwanted switching to other competitors by existing customers.

■ *Diversity.* Where an industry has many companies of equal size and competitive position, rivalry will be more intense. Entry from difference sources, such as the Internet, will also increase rivalry.

Strengths

Five Forces Analysis will help you to identify the main sources of competition and their respective strengths and to build a strong market position based on competitive advantage.

This technique, in fact, provides the raw analytical framework necessary to develop a strategy that will help insulate your company from competitive forces and provide it with competitive advantage. Additionally, it is a good technique for understanding industry evolution, as it will allow you to identify windows of opportunity to capitalise on changes in any of the five forces.

Central to this technique, particularly when trying to understand how an industry will evolve, is the identification that a change in one force will affect the other forces, which may result in the alteration of an industry's structure and its boundaries. This analysis can then:

■ forecast future changes in each of the five competitive forces

■ discover how these changes will affect the other forces

■ discover how the interrelated changes will affect the future profitability of the industry

■ discover the strength of your company's position in this evolved industry

■ discover how you might change the strategy to exploit the changing industry structure.

The Five Forces model will also assist you with long-range planning, as it will focus your attention on the mutual dependency between the industry forces that change over time and the fact that a business strategy should both reactively defend against and actively manage these forces.

Weaknesses

The main weakness, according to critics of the Five Forces model, is that it underestimates the core competencies or capabilities that may serve as a company's competitive advantage in the long term. Industry structure is one factor that determines a company's profitability; others such as unique organisational resources will be important as well. The model is designed to analyse individual business unit strategies within unique industries. It does not take into account the synergies and interdependencies within a corporation's overall portfolio.

Strict interpretations of the model do not fully recognise the importance of social and political factors within or impacting on each of the five forces. For example, the role and influence of government as an industry stakeholder, which some argue should be treated as a separate sixth force, can directly impinge on the competitive parameters of the industry.

Porter himself has acknowledged that the Five Forces model is primarily concerned with what makes some industries, and some positions within them, more attractive – but it does not directly address why or how some companies are able to get into advantageous positions in the first place and why some are able to sustain these positions over time while others are not.

The implicit advice the Five Forces model delivers for formulating strategy may direct a company to focus on industry-level characteristics, encouraging it to allocate resources on influencing the industry's structure even though it may not uniquely benefit from the changes, but may also allow competitors to benefit from them. This course of action may be justifiable if industry structure is the dominant determinant of company performance.

How to do it

Applying the Five Forces model involves three major steps and several substeps, described in the following sections.

Step 1: Collect information

The first step involves specifically identifying your industry. This is not always easy to do and can require you to try several means, including looking at existing demand and supply patterns around specific products and services, using pre-existing classification sources such as the

International Standard Industrial Classification system (also known as the standard industrial classification or SIC), or gaining agreement from business experts familiar with your competitive context. Once the industry is identified, you will need to collect information to identify the characteristics of each of the five forces (see Figure 7.1) and then examine and assess their impact on the industry.

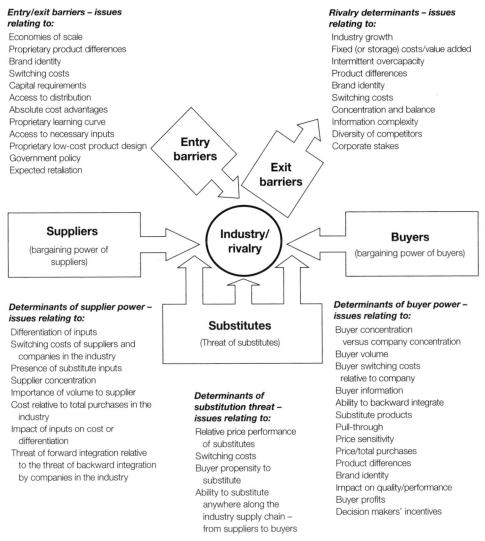

Entry/exit barriers – issues relating to:
Economies of scale
Proprietary product differences
Brand identity
Switching costs
Capital requirements
Access to distribution
Absolute cost advantages
Proprietary learning curve
Access to necessary inputs
Proprietary low-cost product design
Government policy
Expected retaliation

Rivalry determinants – issues relating to:
Industry growth
Fixed (or storage) costs/value added
Intermittent overcapacity
Product differences
Brand identity
Switching costs
Concentration and balance
Information complexity
Diversity of competitors
Corporate stakes

Entry barriers

Exit barriers

Suppliers
(bargaining power of suppliers)

Industry/ rivalry

Buyers
(bargaining power of buyers)

Substitutes
(Threat of substitutes)

Determinants of supplier power – issues relating to:
Differentiation of inputs
Switching costs of suppliers and companies in the industry
Presence of substitute inputs
Supplier concentration
Importance of volume to supplier
Cost relative to total purchases in the industry
Impact of inputs on cost or differentiation
Threat of forward integration relative to the threat of backward integration by companies in the industry

Determinants of substitution threat – issues relating to:
Relative price performance of substitutes
Switching costs
Buyer propensity to substitute
Ability to substitute anywhere along the industry supply chain – from suppliers to buyers

Determinants of buyer power – issues relating to:
Buyer concentration versus company concentration
Buyer volume
Buyer switching costs relative to company
Buyer information
Ability to backward integrate
Substitute products
Pull-through
Price sensitivity
Price/total purchases
Product differences
Brand identity
Impact on quality/performance
Buyer profits
Decision makers' incentives

Figure 7.1 Industry analysis
Source: Adapted from Porter, M.E., *Competitive Advantage: Creating and Sustaining Superior Performance* (London: Collier Macmillan Publishers, 1985).

While much of the information required in this step can be obtained from published sources, it is important to use human sources where possible to improve the objectivity of your analysis and to identify possible market intentions. This process requires you to identify the main sources of competitive pressures, which are:

- rivalry among competitors
- threat of substitute products
- threat of potential entry
- bargaining power of suppliers
- bargaining power of buyers.

Step 2: Assess and evaluate

The second step involves assessing and evaluating the five forces in light of your organisation's and other rivals' competitive ability. This includes determining the direction of the force (that is the arrow) around the industry and the relative strength of each force by giving each of them a value, indicating if it is strong, moderate or weak. One way to do this is to use a scale of 1 to 5, with 1 indicating a weak force and 5 indicating a strong force (see the case studies at the end of this chapter). An important input into this process is providing a logical explanation of how each competitive force works and its role in the overall competitive picture.

For example, the competitive environment is unattractive and profitability will be harder to achieve when rivalry is strong, competition from substitutes is strong, entry barriers are low, and suppliers and buyers have considerable bargaining power.

The competitive environment is attractive and profits more easily generated when rivalry is low to moderate, there are no good substitutes, entry barriers are relatively high, and suppliers and buyers have poor bargaining power. The returns earned by rivals in these attractive industries should be greater over a designated span of years than those earned by rivals in unattractive ones.

A company whose strategy and market position demonstrates a good understanding of these five forces can earn above average profits, even when some or all of the five forces are strong.

The ultimate goal of most business or competitive analysis is to identify the ability of your company to successfully compete within its industry, given the collective strength of the five forces. A comparison of your company's resource strength with regard to the size of the 'fit' gap with each of these five forces will provide valuable insight on strategic opportunities and threats.

Step 3: Develop strategy

The third step requires repeating the first two steps in light of industry change and evolution. To improve the usefulness of this analysis, long-term industry trends should be analysed to determine whether the profitability of the industry is sustainable and how this will affect your company's competitive position. Trends include, among other things, proposed government legislation and regulations, social and consumer trends, international changes and trends, guiding economic forces and technological trends.

Now, integrate these long-term trends within the broader context of corporate strategy to find the tightest 'fit' between your company's resources, capabilities and the external environment. This involves three types of strategic scenario: reactive strategy against likely competitor moves; proactive strategy to manipulate changing forces already in motion; and proactive strategy to explicitly force change in one or all of the five forces.

Industry structure fundamentally affects strategic choices. Understanding how an industry will evolve provides important direction for selecting and managing strategy around these five criteria. Each competitive force should be constantly monitored for its impact on your overall company strategy and the opportunities it represents for extending competitive advantage. The interactions amongst these forces and trends must also be kept in consideration.

Finally, not all industries are alike – for companies with product portfolios across numerous industries, this technique should be repeated for each industry.

Applying the Five Forces model to the US passenger airline industry

(5 = strongest, 1 = weakest)

Threat of entry – weighting 4

■ Deregulation in the 1980s reduced legislative barriers.

■ High capital intensity, offset to a lesser degree by the ability to lease aircraft and hire ground crews on contract.

▶

■ Limited availability of terminal slots offset to some degree by use of secondary or less-accessible airports.

Threat of substitutes – weighting 3

■ Improved information and communication technologies lessen the need for some forms of physical air travel.

■ Market growth of profitable business class is slowing due to the impact of information technology reducing the need for face-to-face communication.

Bargaining power of buyers – weighting 4

■ Hyper-competition has made air travel more closely resemble a commodity, resulting in overcapacity.

■ Price sensitivity of consumers has not been significantly offset by loyalty programmes.

■ Greater availability of real-time price and other travel factor considerations through presence of air travel sites via the World Wide Web.

■ Sale of tickets directly by existing rivals' websites lessens the need to share rent with travel agents.

Bargaining power of suppliers – weighting 4

■ Increasingly militant unions (flight attendants, machinists, pilots, for example) have eroded the economic rent associated with producer surplus.

■ There are very few suppliers of aircraft for certain forms (trans-oceanic) of long-distance travel.

■ Public entities have been less likely to provide public funding for airport expansion, new landing slots, or larger/more runways.

■ Bankruptcy regulations allow existing competitors to favourably restructure existing contracts and lessen the financial burdens created by some suppliers.

Degree of competitive rivalry – weighting 4–5

■ Market share warfare is the industry norm.

■ Some long-standing carriers, particularly the full-service, long-haul-oriented ones, have folded or gone into bankruptcy.

■ Competition frequently devolves to considerations of pricing.

■ Growth in travel class offset by larger planes and competitive entry, resulting in overcapacity and lower margins.

■ High proportion of fixed costs and resulting variable cost pricing through heavy discounting to maximise the contribution margin from excess capacity.

■ High exit barriers for larger, more heavily invested carriers.

Conclusion: All the competitive forces are at least moderately strong and in some cases very strong. The attractiveness of the airline industry is low, and it will generally be difficult to sustain attractive levels of profitability in light of the current set of forces. However, despite this, some airlines have managed to create strategies that effectively offset many of the negative forces and achieve reasonable levels of profitability, reinforcing the need we previously described to develop effective strategies in light of the forces and trendsimpacting them.

Applying the Five Forces to the global pharmaceutical drug industry

(5 = strongest, 1 = weakest)

Threat of entry – weighting 3

■ High capital requirements (average drug requires $200 million in R&D) and substantial unrecoverable marketing expenditures.

■ Hence, niche strategies are the only feasible basis of competition for new entrants that, if successful, are frequently subject to aggressive takeover overtures.

■ High degree of specialised expertise required to successfully participate over the long run.

■ Patent protection promotes and protects innovation.

Threat of substitutes – weighting 2

■ Few substitutes exist for drug therapy, and it is often much cheaper than hands-on medical and surgical interventions.

■ Generic products only available after lengthy period of patent protection disappears.

■ Other forms of therapy remain less trusted and are typically more risky from a scientific viewpoint than pharmaceuticals.

Bargaining power of buyers – weighting 1–2

■ Doctors, rather than patients, usually make the purchase decision based on product attributes and efficacy, not price.

■ When consumers do make the purchase decision, they show a high brand loyalty that works against private-label drugs.

■ Some organised buying groups (health maintenance organisations, public bodies such as healthcare providers, and so on, for example) have, to a degree, eroded the discretionary powers of pharmaceutical manufacturers.

Bargaining power of suppliers – weighting 2

■ Many of the raw inputs to pharmaceuticals are commodities.

■ Biotechnology and gene therapy are still in the developmental stage.

■ Many of the promising new biotech companies have or will be acquired by established drug companies.

■ Highly specialised human resources can be difficult to acquire in some pharmaceutical therapy areas.

Degree of competitive rivalry – weighting 3

■ Continual product innovation by rivals creates new or growing demand.

■ Aging baby boomers and growing life spans will foster growth.   ▶

■ A high percentage of unrecoverable costs such as R&D, marketing and distribution increase barriers to exit.

■ Offsetting the effect of high premiums offered by incumbents for acquisitions of smaller companies.

Conclusion: All of the competitive forces now facing this industry are fairly weak to moderate. The attractiveness of the industry remains good, and the profitability of rivals in the drug industry is relatively high. The analyst must be careful to consider existing and potential trends that may impact the forces and their interactions, a task that may show that future attractiveness and profitability may be relatively harder for pharmaceutical companies to achieve in future years.

Endnote

[1] See Porter, M.E., *Competitive Strategy: Techniques for Analyzing Industries and Competitors* (London: Collier Macmillan Publishers, 1980).

8

Issue analysis

Description and purpose

Issue analysis aids the strategic and competitive intelligence (CI) efforts of companies by helping them anticipate changes in their external environments and to become more proactive in shaping it through their influence on public policy (PP). It is also a useful technique for a company to use to position itself to deal with changes in public policy. The opinions of stakeholders can affect corporate decisions related to consumer protection, environmental protection, financing options, health and safety, marketing, operating standards, product packaging and placement, and site location, among others.

Public environmental intelligence provides early warning of threats and opportunities emerging from the global PP environment that can affect a company in achieving its strategy. Public environment intelligence can be used in a variety of decision-making areas, including:

- *creating, changing or defeating legislation or regulation* – for example, enabling Sunday retail sales, modification of tariff regimes, and compliance scheduling timetables

- *changing operating standards to adapt to evolving PP* – companies such as YouTube can broadcast clips of cable or network shows using new web-enabled technologies

- *altering employee performance procedures or labour practices to adapt to PP issues* – for example, providing benefits to same-sex couples, not using under-age contract employees in less developed countries, and providing equal opportunity to employment or advancement regardless of one's demographics

■ *changing the company's mission or taking a leadership role in PP issues* – for example, chemical companies' responsible care initiatives in voluntarily phasing out controversial practices ahead of legal standards

■ *taking a public communication stance on key policy issues* – for example, several large Internet companies vocally addressing privacy and free speech issues

■ *changing vendors or suppliers as a result of PP* – for example, US retailer Wal-Mart establishing a preference policy of purchasing from local suppliers in countries where it has retail stores, when it could be done competitively

■ *entering or exiting product or service lines to adapt to PP issues and standards of liability or public expectations* – for example, Internet service providers refusing to host 'hate' or terrorist-oriented sites, former defence-related companies moving into commercial areas connected to their former contracts, and the sale of products being banned in one country to countries where the bans are not similarly legislated.

Issue analysis is also part of the larger (strategic) issue management process. The strategic purpose of issue analysis is to assist decision makers in identifying, monitoring and selecting issues for action that may affect the company's profitability and competitiveness. It helps strategic decision makers to avoid surprises that emerge from change in the broad environmental STEEP factors and to better address STEEP issues, regardless of whether they are opportunities or threats (see Chapter 11 for more on STEEP analysis).

There are several key lessons you need to note when utilising issue analysis:

■ the time over which an issue develops can vary enormously; sometimes it can develop in days or weeks, sometimes in years or even over decades

■ many issues will get transformed as they evolve – there are many twists and turns among issues and stakeholders in the PP-making process that can shift the expected trajectory of an issue. This makes planning and the consideration of different scenarios (see Chapter 10) paramount

■ there is uncertainty surrounding which issues will actually make it onto the PP arena. Some issues are best resolved through proactive measures, while selected others can be safely ignored in the decision-making process.

Strengths

Conducting issue analysis can enhance a company's competitiveness through improved strategic decision making based around proper researching PP and STEEP factors. It gives management the advantage of selecting the highest impact issues that the organisation should respond to, as opposed to being distracted by lower impact issues and needlessly wasting valuable resources.

Issue analysis also helps in the early identification of emerging issues, thus providing lead time to coordinate internal organisational and external environmental responses. It can reduce the risk and uncertainty of adapting organisational initiatives in a changing environment. It promotes the management of issues rather than reactions to them.

The active monitoring and addressing of issues helps the company to deflect concerns before they become major problems and to transform emerging trends into corporate opportunities. It provides an organisation-wide process for anticipating and dealing with STEEP factors, enabling the company to be in tune with societal expectations and avoid serious public mistakes that could harm its credibility and reputation with critical stakeholders.

Weaknesses

Although issue analysis can be beneficial to organisations in several ways, its applicability and usefulness is constrained by several factors. The most common of these include the following:

■ It is a helpful tool for organisations facing PP challenges, but it might not always assist them in achieving a competitive or strategic advantage. This is because some issues are institutional by nature and must be dealt with by the entire industry or the largest competitors, thereby not providing the kinds of differential advantages companies often seek in making resource allocations.

■ It must be carried out on an ongoing basis. For this to happen, inputs must be generated by regular monitoring and scanning of the company's environment. This is difficult for most companies not only due to the overwhelming amount of data available in the environment but also because of the difficulties of selecting the important data.

■ Many issues defy logical or rigorous assessment because they contain emotional or attitudinal factors, often due to media attention, which make their evolution difficult to predict.

■ There are few yardsticks with which to evaluate the effectiveness or success of the issue analysis process. This can lead to the under-allocation of resources, even though many managers recognise that it is important regardless of the unreliability of results.

■ It is difficult to see direct correlation between intervening in issues and resultant financial or market measures.

How to do it

The task in issue analysis is to take the environmental data gathered during scanning and monitoring, and to sort it into informational categories, rank it, evaluate it according to selected criteria, and draw conclusions for managerial decisions. Experts suggest that three tasks are precursors to effective issue analysis:

■ issue identification and forecasting

■ issue analysis and assessment

■ selection of issues – response patterns and types.

Step 1: Issue identification and forecasting

Before an issue can be analysed, it has to be identified. The techniques listed here are some of the more popular ones for identifying issues.

■ *Content analysis.* This technique involves scanning newspapers, web logs, journals, books, articles, reports, newsletters, speeches and so forth. The approach and the results can be either quantitative or qualitative.

■ *Scenario development.* Scenarios are written descriptions of plausible alternative futures based on specified assumptions about relevant environmental forces (frequently categorised as STEEP) and their interactions. We describe this in greater depth in Chapter 10.

■ *Survey techniques.* The major techniques in this category include public and stakeholder opinion polling, attitudinal surveys and Delphi panels. Delphi panels use a sequence of questionnaires distributed to experts in which the responses to one questionnaire are used to produce successive questionnaires. Any set of information available to some experts and not to others is passed along, allowing each person on the panel to have the same information to produce his or her forecast. Delphi panels improve the use of expert opinion through polling based on anonymity, statistical display and feedback of reasoning.

The actual issue analysis process then consists of three components:

■ forecasting

■ assessment

■ selection of issues to allow the organisation's decision makers to determine the nature of potential responses.

The first step is to anticipate or forecast the development of the issue that your organisation monitors. Several tools that can assist you with this are described below.

Four-stage life cycle progression of PP issues

One particularly helpful tool for forecasting the sequence and development of issues is known as the *issue life cycle*. It is based on the premise that issues tend to evolve through a fairly logical progression from when they first appear on the company's radar screen until they are no longer prevalent in the company's environment.

Two caveats should be noted in using the issue life cycle:

■ issues can be derailed at almost any stage of the life cycle by other matters, as other issues grow in attention, as political or social attention shifts, as media coverage of them declines, or when interest groups and stakeholders take effective actions that either accelerate or impede progress

■ the amount of time between issue stages can vary a great deal from country to country, government to government, and issue to issue.

As issues evolve, public attention increases until a peak point is reached, while managerial discretion steadily decreases. Following are the four common stages through which PP issues progress.

1 *Formation*. Issue development usually signals structural changes and gives rise to the recognition of an issue. It is often difficult to identify the subtle, often imperceptible, changes that occur in societal expectations at this stage. Often, the observations of certain stakeholders (academics, authors, government sponsored researchers, media commentators, public crusaders, PP researchers, think tanks or

web commentators) can be helpful in identifying expectation shifts. It is usually best for a company to attempt to influence the evolution of an issue at this early stage, when it is easier to set the boundaries and terms of the debate.

2 *Politicisation*. This stage sees the creation of a special set of stakeholders known as *interest groups*, who want to see the issues resolved. They frequently try to get the issue placed on the PP agenda for consideration by public bodies. Specific remedies will start to emerge during debate. A company has less control over shaping the issue at this stage but can still have an influence if it is willing to take an active role.

3 *Legislative formalisation*. This is the stage at which the issue has peak public attention. It is defined in more concrete terms (operational and legal) and frequently results in new legislation or regulations being introduced. This is usually the last chance the company has to influence the development of an issue, and any changes at this stage are usually costly, and require heavy lobbying, grassroots activity and public communications.

4 *Regulation/litigation*. At this stage, public attention plateaus, enforcement procedures become routine, and penalties apply to those who violate the law. It is now even more difficult and costly for a company to effect change in the issue.

Figure 8.1 provides a view of the issue life cycle and shows how the four-stage model evolves. It also shows the nature of the discretion available to the organisation as it determines when it will respond to the issue, depending on where it is in the cycle.

Seven-stage progression of PP

The four-stage model just described is not the only one you can use to understand the evolution of issues. You can also identify the development of issues through the following seven stages:

1 *The problem*. The public feel general dissatisfaction over events in the STEEP environment, although they may not yet have reached consensus as to what the problem is.

2 *The label*. This is where a stakeholder, usually an interest group, addresses the issue and is able to attach a label to it.

3 *Crystallisation*. The media get wind of the issue and promotes it in the public arena. The reason for the problem is now clear.

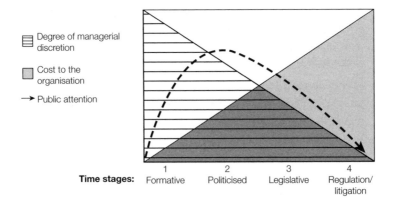

Time stages: | 1 Formative | 2 Politicised | 3 Legislative | 4 Regulation/litigation

Strategic dimensions of public issues

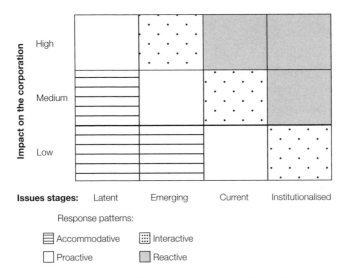

Issues stages: Latent   Emerging   Current   Institutionalised

Response patterns:

⊟ Accommodative   ⊞ Interactive

☐ Proactive   ▨ Reactive

Figure 8.1 Decision-oriented applications of the issues life cycle model
Source: Adapted from Bucholz, R.A., *Business Environment and Public Policy: Implications for Management*, 5th edn (Upper Saddle River, NJ: Pearson Education, Inc., 1995).

4 *Solutions.* Numerous solutions to the problem emerge as the media continues to fan the issue. An affected company should be involved in shaping the agenda by now, as it will have little opportunity to realistically do so later.

5 *Legislation.* Political leaders get involved in the issue. They propose laws to address it. It now goes in the directions called for by public officials.

6 *Implementation.* The newly passed laws are implemented by government agencies or departments. Legal action through the courts may take place if stakeholder groups perceive that the implementation is not in the spirit of the legislation.

7 *New problems arise.* New issues often grow out of the solutions to older ones. This can often start the cycle over again. Over- and under-regulation are examples of where issues get recycled.

Issue expansion map approach

Then there is the issue expansion map approach, which identifies how an issue expands and how various stakeholders get involved. It consists of four groups:

- *Identification groups.* These are the first to become involved as the dispute expands beyond original participants. They are relatively powerless unless they consolidate with other groups.

- *Attention groups.* They tend to be organised around a small set of issues important to their membership. They are easily mobilised and have resources and access to the media, giving them power to expand the issue beyond their membership.

- *Attentive public.* These are well-educated and well-read members of the public in which are found society's opinion leaders.

- *General public.* Issues expand to this group because either the organisation did not contain the issue at the attention-group level or because the issue is relevant and symbolic to them – or both.

Issue timing approach

Another useful way to classify issues is according to timing, for which there are four major categories of issues:

- *Latent issues.* These are issues that are still not widely discussed in the media or by activist groups and other stakeholders. The scanning of these issues should focus on detecting if pressure is building, which might make the issue more important in the future.

- *Emerging issues.* These are PP questions that have three underlying characteristics:

  - the issue is still evolving as are the positions of the contending parties

  - the issue is likely to be the subject of formal government action in the next few years

■ the issue can still be influenced by the organisation.

■ *Current issue*. This is being debated or otherwise acted on within governmental institutions. specific policies to resolve the issue are being legislated and debated by elected or appointed officials.

■ *Institutionalised issue*. PP has been formulated and adopted as an attempt to resolve the issue. Approved policies are being implemented, most likely within a government agency or department.

Each of the approaches identified above for Step 1 is equally valid. It is up to you as the analyst to select which one would be most appropriate for your organisational needs.

Step 2: Issue analysis and assessment

Some of the techniques described in Step 1 can also be used to help you assess issues, especially Delphi panels and scenario development. Several other techniques are frequently used for analysing and assessing issues, the most popular of which are discussed in the following sections.

Issues distance approach

One approach is to look at issues based on the distance between the organisation and the issues under consideration. Issues would then be identified into three broad categories:

■ *Current issues*. These are already under consideration by PP makers (Stage 3 of the issue life cycle – see Figure 8.1), and organisations are forced to react to them.

■ *Emerging issues*. These are still forming (moving from Stage 1 to Stage 2 of the issue life cycle) and are likely to be coming onto the formal PP-making agenda in the form of legislation in the near future. The company can still influence these issues by proactive and pre-emptive public affairs actions.

■ *Societal issues*. These are vague and frequently remote concerns that may or may not affect business interests in the future. For the time being, and until they become better understood, they are not issues with which the company should be actively concerned.

Issue impact approach

Another approach is to base the classification of the identified issue on the number of people affected, the severity and immediacy of impact of the issue, and the cost of solving the problems relating to the issue. The use of these three criteria results in the following classification:

■ *Universal issues*. These issues affect a large number of people, have a direct and personal impact on them, and are viewed as being serious. They are usually not of a permanent nature and are characterised by such events as energy and inflationary crises or a regional uprising by small groups. In these cases, the public generally looks to government for a quick solution.

■ *Advocacy issues*. These are issues for which the public seeks governmental action to resolve. They are usually complex and build steadily over time. Issues such as the deregulation or regulation of certain industries, the provision of child daycare facilities or foreign investment guidelines commonly fit into this category.

■ *Selective issues*. These issues typically concern specific stakeholder groups. They usually generate costs to the public, but the benefits tend to go to the stakeholder groups who promoted the issue. The stakeholders tend to be identifiable by characteristics such as demography (for example, the unique job and retirement concerns held by baby boomers), geography (for example, urban dwellers concerned about the provision of satisfactory schools in run-down inner city areas), occupation (for example, the provision of benefits to migrant workers) or sector (for example, the protection of certain forests from logging activity).

■ *Technical issues*. These issues are generally not well known nor a concern to most members of the public. Experts or specialists are most concerned about these issues, and they usually end up being settled within the regulatory framework.

Issues priority, leveraging and scoring matrices

Given the large number of issues in an organisation's environment, you need to make an assessment of all the issues in order to recommend to decision makers which ones should be selected for action and resource allocation. Because all organisations have limited resources, efforts should be made to determine where the organisation's actions produce the greatest positive effects overall.

To guide you through this process, there are several important questions that you need to answer:

■ Where is the issue in its stage of development?

■ How probable is it that the issue will evolve so that a government body will legislate on it and cause the issue to have a material impact on the organisation?

■ What is the likely effect of the expected PP on the organisation's profitability?

■ Does the organisation have the capabilities to influence the issue evolution process or the range or nature of possible governmental responses?

Answering these questions requires taking the list of issues generated within the identification phase and placing them in the cells of a matrix bounded by the selection of two variables. Among the variables most frequently used are *probability* (the likelihood that the issue will occur) and *impact* (the severity of the possible effect of the issue). These are often combined into a 3 × 3 matrix, with the variables ranging from high to medium to low, resulting in nine cells, each of which suggests a different priority for subsequent action on behalf of the company. Common versions of this matrix are presented in Figure 8.2.

Step 3: Selection of issues – response patterns and types

A company's response to an issue needs to be a coordinated and planned set of actions, some of which may be internal and some of which will occur in the external or PP environment. It is helpful to consider these response patterns in making an action recommendation to the organisation's decision makers. There are several ways that an issue may be responded to by an organisation, including the following:

■ The organisation could alter its behaviour, that is, its policies or activities, in such a way as to reduce or eliminate the pressures stakeholders are feeling. Johnson & Johnson did this in the USA with the packaging and sealing of its pain medication, Tylenol, after it was discovered that it had been tampered with. One positive side effect of proactive behaviour such as this was that the company may have preempted regulation requiring it to take costlier or possibly less effective steps.

■ The organisation might try to bring its stakeholders' expectations of corporate behaviour and performance closer to its own perceptions of its behaviour and performance.

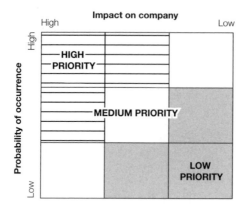

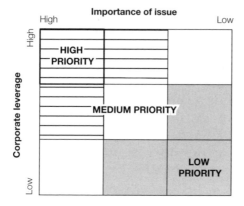

ISSUE PRIORITY MATRIX		
Control	Limited control	No control

High
Medium   Issue power
Low

Figure 8.2 Issues priority, leveraging and scoring matrices
Source: Adapted from Gollner, A.B., *Social Change and Corporate Strategy: The Expanding Role of Public Affairs* (Stamford, CT: Issues Action Publications, 1983); Sopow, E., *The Critical Issues Audit, The Issue Management Workbook Collection* (Leesburg, VA: Issues Action Publications, 1994).

■ The organisation could enhance its stakeholder communication and educational efforts about its activities and policies in the public arena. This is frequently done today using web-based technologies and communication channels.

■ The organisation may contest the issue in the public opinion arena. This could be done through lobbying government decision makers, using the court system and legal challenges, applying grassroots pressure to the issue, or through advocacy advertisements and editorials.

■ The organisation could ignore the issue and hope it goes away or that time might resolve the matter in its favour.

Table 8.1 presents a political issues alternative matrix. It suggests that there are two dimensions to consider when planning a response to an issue. The first dimension is whether a direct or indirect mode of attack should be launched, while the second dimension looks at whether the focal unit of analysis should be an issue for the organisation.

Table 8.1 Political issues alternatives matrix

Mode of attack	Orientation	Group
Direct	Defuse the issue	Attack the group
Indirect	Blur the issue	Undermine the group

Source: Adapted from Mahon, J., 'Corporate political strategy', *Business in the Contemporary World*, Autumn, 1989, 50–62.

Four different tactics arise from these two dimensions, as follows:

■ *Defuse the issue.* This is a symbolic action that lacks real substance; for example, it might require the organisation to set up a special committee to look into the issue, fire the leader or say it will change its action/policy amid publicity with no intention of doing so.

■ *Blur the issue.* Bring in other stakeholders, add issues, refine the current issue, postpone action while awaiting more research or discuss all the reasons (constraints) why it cannot comply or respond.

■ *Attack the group.* This is a riskier tactic where an organisation raises questions about the legitimacy of an individual or group in an attempt to discredit them.

■ *Undermine the group.* Co-opt stakeholders, bypass the leadership by making direct appeals to members and use secondary sources of influence.

Another alternative classification scheme for preparing responses to public issues addresses whether the organisation can resist, bargain, capitulate, terminate or cease the activity that has brought about the issue. See Table 8.2 for examples of where each of these strategies and tactics are used.

Table 8.2 Strategies and tactics for political response

Strategies	Tactics	Examples
Resistance	Persuace and propagandise	Ford and Pinto
	Deny responsibility	Nestlé and Infant Formula
		Ford Explorer rollovers
	Question other stakeholders' legitimacy	Tobacco industry
	Countercharge and diversionary tactics	Discrimination against smokers
Bargaining	Positive inducements	Union Carbide and the town of Institute, West Virginia
	Negative inducements	Medical practitioners withholding their services in order to force policy changes
Capitulation	Concede; seek best solution or exoneration	J&J and Tylenol
		P&G and Rely Tampon
Termination	Cease relationships with external stakeholders	GD Searle and IUD
		Levis staying out of China
Cessation	Dissolve the organisation	File bankruptcy

Source: Adapted from Mahon, J., 'Corporate political strategy', *Business in the Contemporary World*, Autumn, 1989, 50–62.

- *Total resistance.* The organisation refuses to change, repulses all challenges or forces the environment to change or adapt to its goals.
- *Bargaining.* The organisation bargains or compromises so that adjustments on all sides are required.
- *Capitulation.* The organisation ends the bargaining with external actors, seeks a replacement or changes its environment, all the while seeking the best solution for itself and exoneration.
- *Termination.* The organisation ends the relationship with the external group and seeks a replacement.
- *Cessation of activity.* The organisation, unwilling or unable to adapt or respond to the changes demanded, disbands.

The eventual outcome of issue analysis is the determination of a handful of issues that would be most important for the organisation to act upon.

Although we have provided several ways of identifying, classifying and prioritising issues, we do not want to suggest that the process does not contain a good degree of subjectivity. This is largely due to the perceptions of uncertainty and risk that are always prevalent in the issue environment.

The issue identification, analysis and response process rarely unfolds in the linear, sequential fashion described in this chapter.

In the chaotic STEEP environment in which organisations operate, issue analysis and management are multilayered, iterative, trial and error processes that must continuously adapt to evolving conditions. Uncertainty is ever present. However, it is clearly possible to do better than competitors by learning and applying some of the tools discussed in this chapter.

Issues priority assessment process at Minnegasco

Minnegasco (now part of CenterPoint Energy), an American gas utility company operating in Minnesota, has an issue analysis process in place. When looking at their issues, their specialists rate the external forces that can impact the company's success with factors such as the credibility of the groups initiating the proposal, the opposition's strengths and weaknesses, the impact on the state's budget, the positions of the governor and relevant state agencies and their ability (or lack thereof) to get coalitions to work with them.

Once the issues are rated, they then compile an average score for each legislative initiative. That score is weighed against the degree of financial impact to the company, the likelihood for success, and any other public affairs impacts, including the impact the initiative will have on their public affairs relationships. These three elements – chance for success, financial impact and public affairs impact – are taken together and averaged.

During issue analysis, Minnegasco analysts will then ask themselves questions such as:

■ Are we going to harm or improve legislative relationships with this effort?

■ How are other utilities in the industry going to react?

■ How are our customers going to react?

■ What other coalition actions are we going to have to deal with?

Source: Adapted from Sundberg, K. and Shafer, P. (ed.), 'Using the tools of quality to assess state government relations', *Adding Value to the Public Affairs Function* (Washington, DC: Public Affairs Council, 1994), p. 195.

Issues priority rating for Xerox's Washington office

Xerox's Washington office had developed a ranking scheme for identified PP requiring action for which a planned programme could be developed with an identified completion point. The issues relate to areas of interest where Xerox wishes to maintain a degree of activity or awareness. The ranking approach is based on the priority rating: ▶

1   Issue has high potential impact on Xerox and will require a high level of Government Affairs Office activity; may be longer term; a high impact potential requires priority treatment.

2   Less Xerox-specific impact but important enough to require active monitoring; adequately covered by a third-party organisation, but should include Government Affairs Office involvement in third-party activity.

3   Low potential impact for Xerox or very long-term issue with little or no current activity; Government Affairs Office will attempt to monitor but will rely on third parties for active monitoring and input.

9

Product life cycle analysis

Description and purpose

Product life cycle (PLC) analysis describes how sales of a product evolves as a function of time. This model states that, similar to all living organisms, products pass through four stages during their life: introduction, growth, maturity and decline. Taken together, these four stages provide a framework that recommends specific marketing strategies for each PLC stage in order to maximise profitability over the product's life.

The PLC theory has been around for a number of years and is generally attributed to the work of Joel Dean, who wrote about the concept in a 1950 article in the *Harvard Business Review*, entitled 'Pricing policies for new products'.[1]

The product life cycle provides an invaluable perspective to the development of both product and marketing strategies as each phase of the life cycle has distinct characteristics that affect a firm's operation. Different strategies are often required through each stage as customer attitudes and needs, the number of competitors, and market forces change and evolve through the course of the product's life cycle.

The PLC when drawn looks like the bell-shaped logistic curve shown in Figure 9.1(a) and (b).

Stage 1: Introduction

Introduction refers to the development and market introduction of a new product. It is often accompanied by slow sales growth. Prior to introduction, the product may have been in a long period of development and at

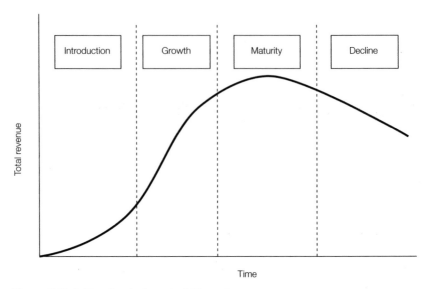

Figure 9.1(a) The classical product life cycle

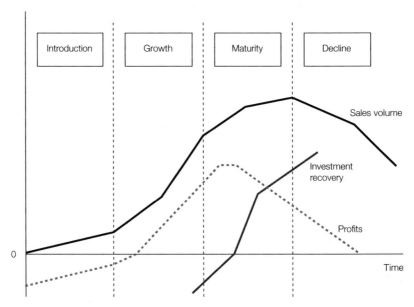

Figure 9.1(b) The product life cycle identifying sales, profits and investment factors

introduction the financial requirements to effectively roll it out can be extensive. When a product is first introduced into the market, it often meets initial resistance from consumers because they are unaware of its existence or they are unsure of its risks and benefits. Hence, only a small proportion of the potential market purchases the product.

Stage 2: Growth

Consumers become aware of the product and its benefits through heavy promotion by the pioneering firm(s). With increasing consumer acceptance, unit sales begin to grow at an increasing rate. During this stage, product and brand differentiation begin as firms start to jockey for competitive advantage. As demand outstrips supply, leading indicators at the wholesale and production levels provide an incentive for more growth than is warranted by retail demand. Typically, sales and profits rise, competitors are attracted, and improved products or imitations enter the market. Eventually, this increased competition leads some of the firms to consider competing on price. This signals the onset of the maturity stage.

Stage 3: Maturity

The profit associated by the growth stage attracts many more competitors to the product market. Market saturation soon ensues, resulting in a sales growth plateau as the majority of potential consumers have already purchased the product. Replacement purchases become the major factor driving subsequent sales. As the maturity stage unfolds, price competition intensifies, ever-finer distinctions between competitive product attributes are made, and promotion and advertising to niche segments within the product market rapidly develop.

Stage 4: Decline

In Stage 4, the industry structure becomes radically altered. Sales begin to rapidly drop from the plateau of the maturity stage as consumers start to buy newer and more innovative products. Overcapacity results in an industry shakeout. Industry concentration is precipitated by severe price competition, mergers and acquisitions, and bankruptcies. Sales continue to decline. The few remaining firms may then decide to take the product off the market. Last but not least, the possibility that the market might actually be impacted through disruptive innovation also suggests that the decline stage may actually serve as a launching off point for the sales of related new products.

These explanations for the shape and stages of the classic PLC curve were enhanced with various strategic prescriptions designed to optimally guide product managers to make better decisions through the various stages. Several generalised strategic prescriptions became routinely associated for each stage of the PLC. They are described below and summarised in Tables 9.1 and 2.

Stage 1: Introduction strategies

Product life cycle theory prescribes a strategy of aggressive promotion during the introduction stage. Heavy investment is required to establish a market by educating consumers about (i) the existence of the product and (ii) the relative benefits of using the product. The main message of marketing efforts should be directed towards convincing potential early adopters of the merits of the product as compared to the status quo of existing products. Typically, PLC theory advocates a selective distribution strategy premised on securing channels used by early adopters. Retail prices are usually set fairly high in order to recover the costs of product investment and development. A generalised manufacturing strategy is employed in order to defer heavy fixed cost investments until a feasible market demand is justified.

Potential strategies available to the organisation at this stage of the PLC:

- *Rapid skimming*. Launching the new product at a high price and with heavy promotion. This strategy attempts to accelerate the rate of market penetration, e.g. the introduction of the Lexus automobile.

- *Slow skimming*. Launching the product at a high price, but using low promotional activity, e.g. Apple i-products. Using this strategy opens the firm to greater potential competition.

- *Rapid penetration*. Launching the product at a low price with heavy promotion. This is a common strategy used for household consumer products.

- *Slow penetration*. Launching the product at a low price with little promotion. This would be characteristic for introductions of products by small businesses.

Stage 2: Growth strategies

During the growth stage, the emphasis switches from a focus on early adopters to the entire market as more customers acquire the product. The marketing strategy now focuses on the firm's proprietary branding attributes. Generally, advertising emphasis will be of medium intensity, as sales growth will normally challenge production capacity even in the absence of intensive advertising. Additionally, during the growth stage, the firm may consider switching its manufacturing strategy to a batch process to support the growing demand. With the increase in demand, most distribution channels will no longer need to be convinced to carry the product.

One of the most important strategic decisions to be made in the growth stage regards pricing strategy. Essentially, the firm can pursue a skimming or penetration pricing policy. A skimming strategy involves setting an initially high price in order to capture the economic rents associated with first mover advantage.

Alternately, the firm may choose to implement a penetration pricing policy. The rationale for pursuing such a pricing policy is to under-price the competition in order to secure a larger market share in the long run as the PLC progresses. Penetration pricing strategy essentially defers profits until the maturity stage when having the lowest cost structure in the market assures high profitability. A penetration strategy assumes that the losses incurred during share building in the growth stage will be more than offset by profits in the maturity stage.

In summary, following acceptance by early innovators, conventional consumers will start following their lead. New competitors are likely to now enter the market attracted by the opportunities for large-scale production and profit. New product features may appear as the market expands. Prices will remain steady or fall only slightly. Profit margins will peak as expenses are spread over a larger volume.

Strategies include:

■ improving quality and adding new features and/or models

■ sourcing new market segments

■ sourcing new distribution channels

■ shifting marketing strategy focus to increase demand

■ lowering prices to attract price sensitive buyers.

Stage 3: Maturity strategies

During this stage, generalised PLC strategy reverts to holding market share as opposed to expansion. Pricing strategy is limited to setting prices in synch with the market's willingness to pay. An important dimension of this stage is the avoidance of initiating a price war in which none of the participants emerge victorious. Price wars will effectively transfer any available producer surplus over to consumer surplus – an outcome that benefits none of the firms involved. It is equally important for the firm to recognise the onset of maturity so as to delay the entry of private label competition into the product market with deterring price reductions. The ultimate pricing strategy in Stage 3 hinges on the selection of a broad strategy for the product market. During the maturity stage, the primary strategic choice is whether to pursue a low-cost-based or differentiation strategy.

Promotional strategy focuses on the distribution channel offering heavy trade discounts to established retailers in order to protect valuable shelf space rather than to attempting to expand distribution channels. Advertising expenditures are moderate and developed to support brand differentiation. More intense during this stage are promotional strategies targeted to consumers to encourage rival's customers to switch brands. To support low costs and consequent margins, manufacturing strategy often switches to assembly line processes to maximise the experience effects associated with higher volumes.

Many firms today operate in a mature market that in itself has three stages:

- growth maturity (sales start to decline due to distribution saturation)
- stable maturity (sales remain level as market saturates)
- decaying maturity (sales decline as consumers move to new products and services).

As mentioned previously, a key feature of this stage is that of over-capacity due to the intensifying competition.

There are three main strategies that can be used here:

- *Market modification.* Looking for new markets and market segments to stimulate increased usage. This strategy may include repositioning the brand.
- *Product modification.* This would address issues of product re-launch, quality improvement, product feature and style enhancements.
- *Marketing mix modification.* Reviewing several elements of the marketing mix such as pricing, advertising and distribution channels. The danger here is that any step would be quickly imitated by the competition.

Stage 4: Decline strategies

The PLC theory essentially offers two strategic choices for managing a product in the decline stage. The first is to exit the product market in order to stem financial losses in a rapidly declining market. The second is to extract as much cash flow as possible with minimal promotional investment. This involves a low pricing strategy in order to ensure that there is no unsold inventory. Unprofitable distribution channels are systematically closed. Advertising, consumer incentive programmes and trade discounts are phased out. Some firms may choose to extend feasible production volumes by acquiring rival firms wishing to exit the market. A common supporting manufacturing strategy in this scenario may be to switch to a continuous flow process in order to achieve minimum cost structures. Eventually, the product sales decline, resulting in eventual removal from the market.

The key problem in this stage is the lack of systematic policies to manage declining products. Management's attention has often shifted to new or mature products. The key actions to be reviewed in the decline stage are:

■ identifying weak products

■ determining whether there are marketing strategies and opportunities still available – this is called a milking strategy

■ deciding whether to abandon the product.

It is the last action that creates a great deal of angst and reluctance. Logic and good analysis plays a key role here as the premature acceptance of product decline often predisposes managers to focus more intensely on new products to the detriment of older established brands. This fixation is fraught with at least two dangers. First, the introduction of new products is extremely resource intensive. Second, the premature neglect of established brands essentially orphans the large investment and valuable consumer goodwill generated from previous brand-establishing campaigns.

Table 9.1 PLC strategies

Strategy	Introduction	Growth	Maturity	Decline
Pricing	Two options: ■ high to offset costs of product launch ■ low to induce adopters	Two options: ■ high – skimming ■ low – penetration	■ Market bearing price ■ Low enough to avoid price war or entry of private label competition	■ Low to reduce risk of unsold inventory
Trade promotion	■ High intensity ■ Heavy discounts	■ Low intensity	■ Heavy promotion to protect shelf space	■ Low intensity ■ Close unprofitable distribution channels
Consumer promotion	■ High intensity and focus on early adopters through samples, coupons, etc.	■ Low to medium intensity as resources shifted to advertising	■ High intensity to induce brand switching form substitutes	■ None
Advertising	■ Focus on product attributes and early adopters	■ Medium intensity focus on mass market and brand attributes	■ Medium intensity to support brand differentiation from substitutes	■ Minimum intensity needed to move inventory
Manufacturing	■ Job process	■ Batch process	■ Assembly line	■ Continuous flow

Source: Adapted from Rowe, A., Mason, R. and Dickel, K., *Strategic Management* (Reading, MA: Addison-Wesley, 1986), p. 156.

Table 9.2 Key characteristics of PLC stages

	Introduction	Growth	Maturity	Decline
Concentration of competitors	High; few pioneers, monopoly	Declining as more competition enters	Increasing industry shakeout	High; few remaining players
Product	One	Variety, brand building	Battle of the brands	Drop out
Product differentiation	Low, if any	Increasing; imitations and variations	High; increasing market segmentation	Decreasing as competitors leave market
Barriers to entry	High, if product can be protected	Decreasing; growth technology transfer	Increasing as capital intensity increases	High capital intensity; low returns
Barriers to exit	Low; little investment	Low but increasing	High for large company	Decreasing; endgame
Price	Skimming or penetration	Meet competition; price dealing/price cutting	Meet competition; price dealing/price cutting	Meet competition; Price dealing/price cutting
Price elasticity of demand	Inelastic; few customers	Increasingly elastic	Inelastic only in segments	Very elastic; bargaining power of buyers high
Ratio of fixed to variable cost	Generally low	Increasing	High	Decreasing
Economies of scale	Few; generally unimportant	Increasing capital intensity	High	High
Experience curve effects	Large early gains	Very high; large production volume	Decreasing magnitude	Few
Vertical integration of competitors	Low	Increasing	High	High
Risk involved in business	Low	Increasing	Increasing	Declining exit barriers

Source: Adapted from: Rowe, A., Mason, R. and Dickel, K., *Strategic Management* (Reading, MA: Addison-Wesley, 1986). p. 156.

Strengths

While the classic bell-shaped PLC discussed above has been validated in some industries, it is only one of many different types of product life cycles. Most of the research done on PLC theory has tended to be limited to consumer products that are frequently purchased, low-priced, and widely distributed.

Despite this lack of empirical support, the PLC continues to make a deep impact on management thought. General acceptance of PLC theory reached its height with its inclusion in portfolio matrix theory in the 1970s. Most notable was the use of the PLC combined with experience curve analysis[1] and as the basis of the BCG growth/share matrix.[2]

In fact, even today, most new marketing textbooks still devote several pages to a discussion of the PLC. In terms of the strategic choice between low cost and differentiation strategy, the PLC has a deterministic bias towards low cost strategy. Perhaps the greatest contribution of the product life cycle to strategy theory was as a contributing basis to evolutionary S curve analysis[3] – a promising theoretical development that deals with shortening product life cycles and the pervasive impact of proliferating innovation in technology.

Ironically, the main weakness of PLC theory may turn out to be its most significant contribution to management thought. By applying diffusion theory to market analysis, the PLC has shed much insight into the demand-side issues of strategy. It appears that research into the PLC has pointed the way forward to exploring the other side of the market dynamic equation – the supply dimension.

Weaknesses

Several implementation issues for PLC analysis present formidable challenges. For example, identifying product distinctions. Are you going to group products via product classes, product forms or product brands? These distinctions are often ambiguous, depend on significant amounts of judgement and will drastically impact the shape and implications of PLC analysis.

Another challenge is the difficulty of distinguishing within which stage a product currently sits. By defining markets too narrowly as a result of a product focus rather than a customer orientation, management often instigates market decline on its own accord.

The PLC may lure some managers into de-emphasising the fact that marketing effort is a significant factor in determining the shape of the PLC. The PLC infers that sales is an independent variable when, in fact, it is the opposite – a dependent variable. Application of the PLC can therefore potentially confuse the cause and effect sequence of dynamic markets.

As mentioned above, the PLC is impacted heavily by marketing effort. The strongest cases in point in support of this are products that rejuvenate after a long period of stability or the persistence of products that have been in the maturity stage for an inordinate period of time without showing any signs of decline. The continued existence and sales acceptance of product brands such as Jell-O desserts, Listerine antiseptic mouthwash, Tide detergents, 7-Up soft drinks, HP sauce, Colman's mustard, Guinness beers, Kleenex tissues, Lyle's Golden Syrup, Maxwell House coffee, and Planter's peanuts challenge the assumptions of the PLC.

Similarly, product classes such as nylon, Scotch whisky, Italian vermouth, French champagne and perfume, and cold breakfast cereal also defy the conventional logic of PLC theory.

The distinguishing features of all of these products is the fact that they satisfy a basic human need and have unique product attributes supported by creative promotion and marketing communications. These characteristics are all the result of effective marketing strategies that help to override any notion of product life cycles. In this regard, consider the impact of a fairly recent Kellogg's marketing campaign: 'Kellogg's Corn Flakes: Taste them again for the very first time.' This campaign was at least part of the reason why cereal manufacturers were successful in expanding the adult cold cereal market – a product market that the PLC would have prematurely slated for decline.

As an analyst it is important that you take into consideration the flaws of PLC. These include:

■ The bias in the PLC to view eventual decline of markets as a certainty. This leads to a self-fulfilling prophecy as the acceptance of maturity and decline fosters generalised strategies that reduce investment and often cause the market decline. Many successful and profitable firms are competing in low growth mature or declining markets.

■ Generalised strategies do not adequately incorporate competitive market dynamics (e.g. differences between large and small firms, established versus new firms, original entry versus market entry through acquisition, licensing, joint venture, or by firms employing different strategies from the firm central to the PLC analysis).

■ The PLC makes no concessions for the fact that, in an established industry, the developed infrastructure makes subsequent product introductions easier, delivering a much higher probability of success.

■ Blind application of the PLC will usually endorse the bias towards a low-cost strategy and does not take into account the effects of experience. Additionally, the PLC theory gives short shrift to the strategic importance of maintaining technology, marketing and manufacturing process flexibility.

How to do it

Step 1: Estimate potential demand

The first step in applying PLC theory is to understand market demand. Market research is required to identify the consumer segment(s), estimate total demand, understand tastes and preferences, identify unmet needs, and gauge the strength of potential and incumbent substitutes. All of the standard tenets of market research apply to this first step and must be analysed to determine where the market exists to support a reasonable probability of success.

Step 2: Determine price range

There are several methods to approximate a competitive price point:

■ *Expert consultation.* Ask internal and external sources to suggest a reasonable price. Engineers, operations managers and other technical staff can offer insights into the technical feasibility of producing the item for a specified price range. Established distribution channels often offer a rich source of information as to the relative value the proposed new product would offer the consumer relative to competitive offerings.

■ *Consumer research.* Many of the standard techniques of consumer research can be used to determine a reasonable price range such as barter equivalent analysis and in-depth interview techniques. These techniques will also give the analyst a rough approximation of price elasticity.

Step 3: Forecast sales for a range of possible prices

Use the concept of customer value analysis[4] to determine the total value of ownership of the proposed product that includes a breakdown of all of the costs and all of the benefits that the product bestows over its life span. This customer value analysis should then be repeated for competing products. Next, use this analysis as a backdrop to compare the relative competitiveness of the new product as compared to potential and incumbent products at the various price points.

Step 4: Consider the risk associated with competitive price cuts

If a product will not compete directly with any substitutes or will only encroach on a small portion of the incumbent's established market, the probability of a competitive price decline will be lower. If, however, the new product is presumed to displace a significant portion of the incumbent's market share, a competitive price cut can be expected and must be incorporated into any pricing and costing decisions to ensure future product profitability.

Step 5: Determine the fundamental market strategy for the growth stage

A fundamental decision must be made at this point in the analysis as to the selection of the targeted market segment. Incorporating the analysis from the previous four steps, the firm must decide to pursue a skimming or market penetration strategy. Although a generalised analysis can never hope to capture all of the potential idiosyncrasies of specific markets, the PLC curve offers these general guidelines for deciding on a skimming or a penetration strategy:

- *skimming strategy*:
    - new product is truly unique
    - total market demand is forecast to be small
    - demand is price inelastic
    - cross elasticity of demand is low
    - promotional elasticity is high
- *penetration strategy*:
    - new product shares many qualities with established products, so that
        - attribute superiority is small
        - high price elasticity of demand

- experience curve effects will probably be realised
- total market demand is expected to be large
- steep experience curve
- high risk of competition.

This selection of a fundamental marketing strategy will determine the pricing strategy over the growth stage.

Step 6: Define the level of aggregation

The level of aggregation between product class, form or brand is vital to PLC analysis. While each level of aggregation will offer you unique insights, practical application criteria usually override theoretical concerns.

Product life cycle research has shown a tendency to favour product form as the best level of aggregation. Product class usually does not reveal any trends because it includes too many different product markets. In addition, product class only shows trends over a very long time period.

Conversely, aggregating around product brands will not reveal trends because their volatility makes them difficult to model properly. If you remember that a product is defined as the application of a particular technology to satisfy a specific need or desire of a customer segment, then the final selection of a product definition depends in large part on your judgement.

Step 7: Forecast turning points

At this stage PLC analysis starts to distinguish itself as separate from traditional marketing strategy. In PLC theory, each cycle stage requires radically different strategies. Thus, implementing strategies offered by PLC analysis hinges on the correct identification of turning points when the product moves from one stage to another.

While there are many business and economic forecasting techniques (e.g. regression analysis, exponential smoothing, leading indicators and market research), all of these techniques extrapolate from past data. Hence, they are useful only for short-term forecasting, and then only as long as the independent variable assumptions do not radically change. Further, they are most useful for predicting turning points in the economy-wide business cycle. For PLC analysis, however, these techniques are not applicable at the micro-level.

What is required are several turning point forecasting techniques. Unfortunately, this is the most difficult part of PLC analysis. Nonetheless, several helpful methods of forecasting these turning points are readily available.

■ *Declining prices.* This indicator of weakening prices will manifest itself in several ways such as reduced retail prices or the increasing prevalence of discounting which are often informally negotiated. The important distinction for turning point analysis is to detect when the magnitude of discounts changes substantially.

■ *Increasing sales resistance.* A weakening market will require increasing sales effort, such as more salespeople, higher frequency of calls, more attention addressed to individual consumer needs and increased time products spend on market floors or on shelves.

■ *Increasing inventories.* Declining market demand usually precedes excessive inventory accumulation. While macroeconomic measures of inventory buildup will indicate a general slowing of economic growth, the analyst needs to focus on inventory buildup in the relevant product market. Sources of information to aid detection include market specific inventory data published by government or available through subscription from private sources. When composing the subsequent time series, the use of a moving average will help prevent misleading temporary aberrations.

■ *Decreasing order backlogs.* Sources of information include company announcements, financial reports, government statistics and trade association data. Again, current data are the most relevant to performing turning point analysis.

■ *Analysis of internal sales data.* Changes in the rate of growth of product sales may indicate the point of inflection on the PLC between the growth and maturity stage. It is recommended that a moving average is employed to remove any distorting temporary aberration from the analysis.

■ *Media analysis.* Turning points are often predicated by negative press and editorial commentary regarding the product.

■ *Bubble syndrome.* Ironically, turning points often occur when market participants unanimously assert that the 'sky is the limit'. Such unbridled optimism often indicates that the market is close to saturation.

■ *Declining brand preferences.* Weakening markets are often preceded by escalating cross-elasticity of demand.

■ *Increasing product standardisation.* Decreasing attribute differentiation may signal a turning point into the maturity stage as commoditisation initiates.

■ *Market entry by private labels*

■ *Market saturation.* Sated market demand is often indicated by an increasing ratio of replacement sales to initial sales.

■ *Common production processes.* One sign of a maturing market may be the uniform adoption of a particular production process indicating an increasing focus on benefiting from experience effects across the industry.

Step 8: Modification of strategy for each stage

The strategies for each stage in the PLC are then implemented in a staged process with the identification of the turning points for each stage of the PLC. Guidance for managing the variables of the market mix in each PLC stage is summarised in Tables 9.1 and 9.2.

Step 9: Remain watchful for a new PLC

The introduction of innovative technology or any other disruptive competitive parameter may precipitate the evolution to a new PLC. In this case, a new PLC analysis will have to be conducted that incorporates these altered assumptions driving the independent analytical variables.

Dupont and nylon

The initial market for nylon was for military applications during the 1940s and 1950s. After product sales began to fall, Dupont, the inventors of nylon, completely ignored PLC theory and boldly targeted the consumer market. Sales soon rejuvenated, as promotional efforts were successful in displacing the incumbent substitute: silk stockings. Sales grew even faster when Dupont's brilliant marketing strategies transformed nylon into an indispensable fashion item. A classic example of marketing creativity and effort forming the PLC and not the other way around.

Kellogg's cold cereal

As the traditional children's market for cold cereal began to decline as baby boomers grew up, traditional PLC theory would suggest exiting the market or at least favouring newer products in the Kellogg stable. Not so for the creative geniuses at Kellogg's. Instead, they intensely promoted ready-to-eat cold cereal as a viable breakfast alternative for adults. The results were astounding as the market increased from $3.7 billion in 1983 to $5.4 billion in 1988 when the 25–49 year age group was consuming

26 per cent more cereal than at the start of the promotional campaign developed by Kellogg's imaginative marketing strategy.

Sources: Adapted from Dhalla, K. and Yuspeh, S. 'Forget the product life cycle', *Harvard Business Review*, January/February, 54(1), 1976,102–111; Varadarajan, P., Clark, T. and Pride, M. 'Controlling the uncontrollable: managing your market environment', *Sloan Management Review*, Winter, 33(2), 1992, 39–50.

Endnotes

1 See Dean, J., 'Pricing policies for new products', *Harvard Business Review*, **29** (November/ December), 1950, 45–53 (reprinted with retrospective commentary in 54(6), 1976, 141–153); and Moyer, R., 'Forecasting turning points', *Business Horizons*, 24(4), 1981, 57–61.

2 See Chapter 20 of the authors' book *Strategic and Competitive Analysis: Methods and Techniques for Analyzing Business Competition* (Upper Saddle River, NJ: Prentice Hall, 2003) for more details about this technique.

3 See Chapter 24 of the authors' book *Strategic and Competitive Analysis: Methods and Techniques for Analyzing Business Competition* (Upper Saddle River, NJ: Prentice Hall, 2003) for more details about this technique.

4 See Chapter 13 of the authors' book *Strategic and Competitive Analysis: Methods and Techniques for Analyzing Business Competition* (Upper Saddle River, NJ: Prentice Hall, 2003) for more details about this technique.

10

Scenario analysis

Description and purpose

A *scenario* is a detailed description of what the future may look like. It is based on a set of assumptions that are critical to an economy's, industry's or technology's evolution. Scenario analysis is a structured way of developing multiple scenarios that address two common decision-making errors – underprediction and overprediction of change. The objective of scenario analysis is to build a shared baseline for strategic thinking and provide strategic early warning.

Companies facing challenges will especially benefit from scenario planning and analysis when the following conditions are present:

- uncertainty is high relative to managers' ability to predict or adjust to the future
- many costly surprises have occurred in the past
- the company does not perceive or generate new opportunities
- the quality of strategic thinking is relatively low
- the industry has experienced significant change or is about to
- the company wants a common language and framework without stifling diversity
- there are strong differences of opinion with multiple opinions having merit
- the company's competitors are using the technique.

Scenario analysis combines quantitative and qualitative analysis that imagines many possible future scenarios of environmental change; it then reduces these scenarios to a manageable number of possibilities; incorporates sensitivity analysis to determine dependent variable relationships; isolates trends and patterns to counteract blind-spots in strategic decision making, and provides a framework for future decisions.

An industry's level of attractiveness (see Chapter 7 for additional information) can change as it evolves over time. Predicting how this evolution will unfold is an uncertain task at best. When uncertainty levels are high, scenario analysis can be a helpful way for decision makers and managers to prepare for the future.

A scenario is a story about possible futures built on carefully constructed plots. Industry scenarios develop detailed, internally consistent descriptions of what the industry could look like in the future. The output of a single scenario is one possible configuration for the industry, while a set of scenarios can be used to encompass a wider range of possible futures. The set can then be used to develop and assess potential competitive actions or movements.

There are four general types of approaches to developing scenarios, and these are described next.

Quantitative method

Computer-generated econometric model

This model attempts to integrate a large number of identified interrelationships between trends. By changing one variable, the downstream effects can be analysed along with effects on the initial variable.

Qualitative methods

Intuitive method

This method rejects the quantitative approach; instead, it stresses the qualitative variables that are thought to disproportionately affect the future. Fundamental trends are identified and projected into the future to try and construct a surprise-free future. This is done by changing some of the trends to explore other possible future outcomes. While this intuitive approach is appealingly simple, the high level of abstraction and lack of systematic application make it less practical and therefore difficult to implement.

Delphi method

In this method, a panel of both internal and external experts is separately questioned (to reduce peer bias) on current and possible future trends in their particular domain of expertise or practice. After several iterations, the results are statistically collated to yield a description of a majority consensus and different opinions. The Delphi approach attempts to determine the sequential causal paths of events and issues that will play out in the future.

Cross-impact analysis

This approach also seeks expert opinion but adds the experts' estimation of the probability and time of occurrence of future trends or events. The result is a probability distribution of the likelihood and timeframe of future events that can be utilised to determine the impact of the removal of one trend or event on the remaining trends or events. Cross-impact analysis focuses on the interrelated dependencies between the various identified events, factors and issues that will impinge on the future.

A mixed scenario analysis is biased toward the qualitative approaches and is a relatively common method employed today. The approach focuses on a qualitative narrative that challenges key assumptions about the future. Initially, a large number of scenarios are developed that are subsequently reduced through either deductive or inductive processes (see Figure 10.1). Through the deductive reduction of the number of factors, the general narrative themes of each scenario are considered, followed by the factors that will be dominant influences in each scenario. Alternately, inductive reduction involves reducing the factors to a manageable number and then projecting potential future values to multiple combinations of these factors to derive plausible scenarios.

Both deductive and inductive methods offer benefits but also carry risks. The deductive reduction process allows the analyst to combine many factors into several narratives that describe the future, but it may omit important combinations of factors; hence, a critical scenario may be missed. Inductive reduction, by first reducing the number of factors, may omit an important variable.

To protect against both of these blind spots, both approaches should generally be pursued. Once a manageable number of inputs has been determined, the scenarios can be subjected to more rigorous analysis.

Regardless of which method of scenario analysis is used, five specific scenario types are usually developed:

■ *STEEP scenario*. This focuses on events external to the company. Less controllable factors are social, technological, economic, environmental and political. The important distinction between a STEEP scenario and a traditional STEEP analysis is that the STEEP scenario incorporates factor dependencies to yield new competitive conditions that would not be readily identified by the STEEP analysis.

- *Sensitivity scenario.* This has the opposite focal scope of a STEEP scenario in that internal factors controllable by the company are the subject of analysis. A common example is the spreadsheet approach used by the finance department.

- *Industry scenario.* This focuses on industry-specific issues and trends, which are relevant to the company's business model. It is distinguished from traditional industry analysis in that it analyses interrelated sequences of trends, events and issues over time.

- *Diversification scenario.* This focuses on industry-specific issues and trends relevant to potential business models the company may pursue in the future, including those associated with merger and acquisition (M&A) prospects. It is essentially exploratory in nature and seeks to identify current and future trends in the company's industry. This type of scenario analysis also envisions the prospects for industry migration.

- *Public issue scenario.* Often companies that are disproportionately exposed to specific public issues or stakeholder-related events will conduct a public issue scenario. For example, an oil company may choose to centre its scenario analysis on energy economics by developing conceivable scenarios of the impact of cartel strength, discovery, conflicts, taxes and so on, of their current and future business models.

The most important factor in the success of any scenario-building programme is the active involvement of top management. This will help to make the seemingly abstract intangibles of scenario analysis more tangible to various members of the management team charged with the responsibility of preparing the company for and making decisions about future competition. Another important success factor is the involvement of analysts from diverse backgrounds. In this regard, analysts with strong backgrounds in the liberal arts, humanities and social sciences can add rich contextual value to the scenario-building process. Everything else being equal, they will be more attuned to the intangible qualitative factors that often have more bearing on future environments than their more technically or quantitatively oriented colleagues. They are also more likely to act as strategic challengers within the scenario development or analysis process by holding contrarian viewpoints.

Strengths

Scenarios can be used to help determine the sources of competitive advantage or critical success factors as industries evolve. The consequences of each scenario can be used to predict competitors' attacking and defensive moves.

The need for internal consistency in scenario analysis forces the analyst to explicitly address the many interrelated sequences and causal paths that may result in conceivable future scenarios. The test of a good scenario is not whether it portrays the future accurately, but whether it enables a company's decision makers to learn, adapt and enrich the ongoing 'strategic conversation'. Through this process of understanding, the company's managers are much better able to grasp the importance of investing in strategic options as a risk contingency strategy. Scenario analysis is one of the best tools to reduce any corporate blind spots about the external environment.

It is also extremely flexible in that the relative degree of quantification/qualification or formal/informal characteristics of the scenario approaches taken can be tailored to the individual company's culture and capabilities.

Although scenario analysis often incorporates forecasting techniques from raw analytical inputs, it goes one step further. Through narrative stories, scenario analysis starts where traditional forecasting ends. By including informal assessments of possible future environments, scenario analysis is able to embrace relevant variables that are beyond the quantitative purview of established forecasting techniques.

Scenario analysis is a useful technique because of its ability to reduce an overwhelming amount of data and information. It is structured to help management understand future competitive environments – this is liberating from a procedural point of view because it is not necessary to capture all of the details. It also improves a company's ability to respond nimbly in rapidly changing environments because it:

- ensures that a company is not focusing on catastrophe to the exclusion of opportunity
- helps a company allocate resources more prudently
- preserves a company's options
- ensures that companies look forward, not backward
- provides companies with the opportunity to rehearse the future.

Weaknesses

A potential shortcoming of scenario analysis occurs when companies use it to replace strategy formulation and planning. Scenario analysis allows a company to see the possible consequences of a predetermined strategy, whether it is the company's current or possible future strategy. As such, this is an analytical technique. While it may support, decompose and formalise a particular strategy, it does not create new strategies.

The tendency to select the scenario that best fits the company's current strengths must be avoided. You need to divorce yourself from this natural tendency and remain objective to the very real possibility of each scenario materialising independent of the company's current competitive position.

The need to get management to agree on scenarios is critical but not always a task that is easy to manage. As scenarios often include both 'soft' and 'fuzzy' as well as quantitative and analytical information, getting people to agree on their labels can require much effort and time. There are always trade-offs to be made in developing simple versus complex scenarios.

Scenarios are also often appealing due to their conceptual simplicity. A difficult trade-off to make in scenario development is that between 'accuracy' and 'direction'. However, getting managers and decision makers to delve deeper into a particular chosen (or base) scenario to understand the level of competitive and financial implications can be difficult, given that most scenarios are constructed at a broad, macro level.

How to do it

Despite its story-like qualities, scenario analysis follows systematic and recognisable phases. The process is highly interactive, intense and imaginative. It begins by isolating the decision to be made, rigorously challenging the mental maps that shape one's perceptions, and hunting and gathering information, often from unorthodox sources.

These phases are summarised in Figure 10.1.

Although there is no single correct way to conduct scenario analysis, several practical guidelines have been developed from collective experience with this approach. The process we describe next for developing scenarios is the one promoted most notably by Schoemaker.[1]

Phases   1   2   3   4

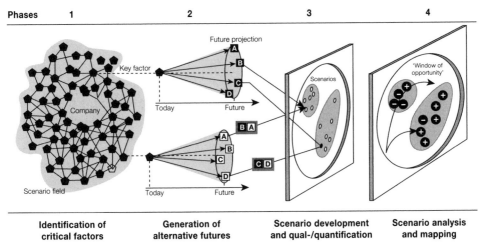

Identification of	**Generation of**	**Scenario development**	**Scenario analysis**
critical factors	**alternative futures**	**and qual-/quantification**	**and mapping**

Figure 10.1 Four phases of scenario development
Source: Adapted from Fink, A., Siebe, A. and Kuhle, J., 'How scenarios support strategic early warning processes', *Foresight*, 6(3), 2004, 173–185.

1 *Define the scope of the analysis.* Set the timeframe and the scope of the analysis in terms of products, markets, customer groups, technologies or geographic areas. The timeframe is dependent on several factors, including industry or product life cycles, political elections, competitors' planning horizons, rate of technological change, economic cycles and so on. Once the appropriate timeframe has been determined, ask what knowledge would be of the highest value to your company at that point in time.

2 *Identify the major stakeholders.* What parties will have an interest in the development of issues of importance in the future? Who will be affected by these parties, and who will affect them? Identify the stakeholders' current roles, interests and power positions and then assess how they have changed over time.

3 *Identify the basic trends.* What industry and STEEP trends are likely to affect the issues you identified in the first step? Briefly explain each trend, including how (positively, negatively or neutrally) and why it influences your company. Those trends in which there is disagreement over their likely continuation are dealt with in the following step.

4 *Identify the uncertainties.* What outcomes and events are uncertain or will significantly affect the issues you are concerned about? For each uncertainty, determine possible outcomes (that is, legislation passed or defeated, or technology developed or not developed). Also attempt to

determine whether relationships exist among these uncertainties and rule out those combinations that are implausible (for example, steadily increasing government and private debt and deficits with steadily declining interest rates).

5 *Construct initial scenario themes.* Several approaches can be utilised, including (i) selecting the top two uncertainties and evaluating them; (ii) clustering various strings of possible outcomes around high versus low continuity, degree of preparedness, turmoil and so on; or (iii) identifying extreme worlds by putting all positive elements in one scenario and all negative elements in another.

6 *Check for consistency and plausibility.* Assess the following: are the trends compatible within the chosen timeframe? If not, remove those trends that do not fit. Next, do the scenarios combine outcomes of uncertainties that indeed fit together? If not, eliminate that scenario. Finally, are the major stakeholders placed in positions they do not like and can change? If so, your scenario will evolve into another one.

7 *Develop learning scenarios.* Some general themes should have emerged from performing the previous steps. Your goal is to identify themes that are strategically relevant and then organise the possible trends and outcomes around these themes. Although the trends appear in each scenario, they should be given more or less weight or attention in different scenarios as appropriate.

8 *Identify the research needs.* You might need to delve more deeply into your blind spots and improve your understanding of uncertainties and trends; for example, consider if you really understand how stakeholders are likely to behave in a particular scenario.

9 *Develop quantitative models.* Re-examine the internal consistencies of the scenarios and assess whether certain interactions need to be formalised via a quantitative model. The models can help to quantify the consequences of various scenarios and keep managers from straying toward implausible scenarios.

10 *Evolve toward decision scenarios.* Iteratively converge toward scenarios that you will eventually use to test your strategies and generate innovative ideas. Ask yourself whether the scenarios address the real issues facing your company and whether they will spur the creativity and appreciation of your company's decision makers.

These steps should ideally culminate in three or four carefully constructed scenario plots. If the scenarios are to function as learning tools, the lessons they teach must be based on issues that are critical to the success of the decision. Only a few scenarios can be fully developed and remembered, and each should represent a plausible alternative future, not a best case, worst case and most likely continuum. Once the scenarios have been fleshed out and made into a narrative, the team identifies their implications and the leading indicators to be monitored on an ongoing basis.

This can also be represented in a scenario matrix as shown in Figure 10.2.

		Environmental uncertainty				
		Development of external scenarios				
		External scenario A	External scenario B	External scenario C	External scenario D	External scenario E
Internal uncertainty	Development of strategy scenarios					
	Strategy scenario 1	+	++	●	++	— —
	Strategy scenario 2	++	+	+	++	++
	Strategy scenario 3	— —	++	+	●	+
	Strategy scenario 4	++	●	— —	●	++
	Strategy scenario 5	—	—	++	+	—

Is the strategic scenario robust against alternative conditions?

Which is the best strategy (scenario) within a specific external development?

Legend: Strong positive correlation ++
Positive correlation +
No impact/neutral ●
Negative correlation —
Strong negative correlation — —

Figure 10.2 Scenario matrix
Source: Adapted from Fink, A., Siebe, A. and Kuhle, J., 'How scenarios support strategic early warning processes', *Foresight*, 6(3), 2004, 173–185.

Once the number of scenario 'plots' has been decided upon, the strategic intent of the company must be determined. It is here that scenario analysis ends and strategic decision making begins. Essentially, three options are open to the company when dealing with future uncertainty:

- *Shape the future.* The most intense stance is for the company to plan to be a shape-shifter by defining the competitive parameters of future scenario(s) by betting on future trends (such as technological discontinuities or the erosion of mobility barriers).

■ *Adapt to the future.* This is a benchmarking approach that puts the company in a position of operational excellence to capitalise on trends as soon as they develop.

■ *Strategic options.* This is a more conservative, proactive strategy that invests the minimal amount necessary to acquire or otherwise purchase strategic options, while avoiding overt vulnerability.

These three strategic opportunities offer different levels of risk and hence different levels of potential reward.

Unlike traditional forecasting or market research, scenarios present alternative images instead of extrapolating current trends from the present. Scenarios also embrace qualitative perspectives and the potential for sharp discontinuities that econometric and other stable-state quantitative models exclude. Consequently, creating scenarios requires managers to question their broadest assumptions about the way the world works so that they can anticipate decisions that might otherwise be missed or denied. Within the company, scenarios provide a common vocabulary and an effective basis for communicating complicated conditions and options.

Good scenarios are plausible and can be surprising, and they should have the power to break old stereotypes. By using scenarios you and your participating colleagues are rehearsing the future; and by recognising the warning signs and the drama that is unfolding, you can avoid surprises, adapt and act effectively. Decisions that have been pretested against a range of possible futures are more likely to stand the test of time and produce robust and resilient plans of action. Ultimately, the end result of scenario analysis is not a more accurate picture of tomorrow, but better decisions today.

Clinical trial disclosure and the impact/probability matrix

An impact/probability matrix was put to use for a group of pharmaceutical industry decision makers who were concerned about clinical trials and their disclosure to the public. In the past, drug companies have been able to conduct clinical trials to learn about the drugs they are developing or marketing, but have been under no obligation to publish their findings.

Over the past couple of years, several events have led government agencies in some countries to call for mandatory disclosure of trial data. Pharmaceutical maker GlaxoSmithKline (GSK) was sued by New York Attorney General Eliot Spitzer in 2004 for fraudulently withholding information on trials on the use of the antidepressant Paxil in children. As part of its settlement, the company is disclosing all trials, regardless of outcome, on a public database. This has spurred many stakeholders, from medical journal editors to the US Congress, to consider permanent, industry-wide, mandatory databases for all trials so that companies can no longer hide unflattering data. Proponents argue that this would improve the access that doctors and patients have to information about drugs.

For the industry decision makers, we used an impact/probability matrix to explore how much disclosure might be mandated and how such mandates would change strategies at pharmaceutical companies. The impact/probability matrix in Figure 10.3 shows how the scenarios played out.

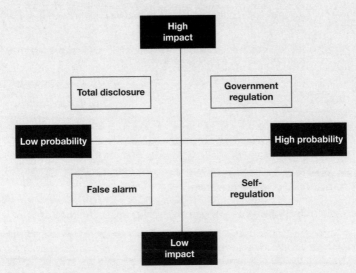

Figure 10.3 Impact/probability matrix

Scenario 1: False alarm – low probability, low impact (flash in the pan)

American business has a short attention span, and there are sometimes fads and short-lived obsessions that quickly disappear. In the *false alarm* scenario, the news cycle churns on, and the media gets tired of discussing something as arcane as clinical trial design and disclosure. Political interest, too, moves on when the election year is over.

In this scenario, the politicians have scored their victories and have moved on to reform industries other than pharmaceuticals. The election year passes, and no political points are left to win. The news media find that the only details of the story left to debate are so specialised and complicated that only pharmaceutical company executives, physicians and FDA regulators are willing to tune in.

This scenario is unlikely, as aging Americans, Medicare budget battles and rising drug costs keep pressure on all aspects of the pharmaceutical business. The public probably will not turn away at this point.

Scenario 2: Self-regulation – high probability, low impact (business as usual)

If no additional major events occur, and pharmaceutical companies decide to increase their own disclosure, the government may allow the industry to police itself ▶

regarding disclosure of information to the public. This is the low-government-intervention scenario – *self-regulation*.

In this scenario, pharmaceutical companies all agree to post the results of completed Phase III clinical trials, which are material to understanding marketed drugs. Phase II and III clinical trials of compounds not yet on the market will be conducted without any requirement for disclosure, though often the investment community will learn of these so as to understand the impacts of product R&D on a company's future.

Scenario 3: Government regulation – high probability, high impact (brewing storm)

The scenario with the greatest likelihood and impact for the industry is where *government regulations* mandate the disclosure of clinical trials.

In this scenario, legal actions continue to pile up, along with continued pressure on the healthcare industry in general.

The voluntary database PhRMA (Pharmaceutical Research and Manufacturers of America) fails to become a useful tool because of a lack of voluntary participation. Public and government discontent continues to grow.

To avoid further legal action, drug companies agree to a government-run database that discloses data on all Phase III clinical trials, regardless of their results. There would be penalties for lack of disclosure.

Scenario 4: Total disclosure – low probability, high impact (wild card)

If there are more scandals involving drug safety or obfuscation of trial data, the public could become so distrustful of the pharmaceutical industry that government agencies might move to demand full registration of all research activities – from preclinical to Phase III trials and through to a new drug application, irrespective of the market potential of the drugs – *total disclosure*.

All participation would be mandatory. Other drug company activities would likely be monitored as well, including what the sales representatives tell prospective customers and how much doctors are paid to provide clinical information.

Business implications of these scenarios

The impact/probability matrix has delineated a range of scenarios, all with varying degrees of disclosure imposed on the pharmaceutical industry.

The next step is to look at the potential impact of these scenarios. A few are listed below:

- *Silence might win*. If the movement toward more public disclosure of drug-trial results is only a flash in the pan, then smart companies will be followers, not leaders. If GSK and Eli Lilly provide a clinical trial database with full disclosure, they will have to live with the potentially negative competitive consequences, while other companies will still have options.

- *Disclosure becomes a way of life*. We could see a new era of government oversight in pharmaceutical industry regulation. There may be new regulatory boards added to government agencies, and companies might need to augment their government relations departments because the regulations are now mandatory.

■ *First to market is not always preferable; fast followers gain new advantage.* The new era of disclosure will change how companies come first to market. It is conventional wisdom that the first to market gets increased brand recognition. Now there is a trade-off. Later entries into markets may be able to structure Phase III trial programs more cheaply because companies will learn from their competitors about blind alleys to avoid.

■ *Learn from every lab in the world.* There will be a loss of secrecy, as competitors can observe trial design, patient populations, endpoints and, eventually, results. Drug companies will be able to reap greater efficiencies as they learn from others. The total cost of drug development could be reduced as competing laboratories avoid duplicating each other's mistakes and improve the design of their clinical trials.

■ *Fewer studies.* Companies may potentially limit studies if all trials must be registered and all results disclosed. A faulty or even exploratory trial design could result in immediate criticism by one's competitors. Post-marketing studies would typically be more open, but head-to-head trials will instantly signal to a competitor an attack on its market share. Head-to-head studies may become riskier, as it would be less possible to conduct trails such as the PROVE IT statin study by Bristol-Myers Squibb, which inadvertently showed the superiority of Pfizer's Lipitor. Pharmaceutical companies may adopt a more targeted approach.

■ *More successful studies.* Even well-designed trials may result in unfavorable results due to poor enrollment, uncertain methodology or endpoints of disease (from side effects through to death) that are not universally accepted. Learning from the experiences of other laboratories could help companies avoid the pitfalls.

Source: Summarised from Garland, E., 'Scenarios in practice: futuring in the pharmaceutical industry', *The Futurist*, January–February, 2006, 30–34.

Endnote

1 Schoemaker, P.J.H., 'How to link strategic vision to core capabilities', *Sloan Management Review*, 34(1), 1992, 67–81; 'Multiple scenario development: its conceptual and behavioral foundation', *Strategic Management Journal*, 14, 1992, 193–213; and 'Scenario planning: a tool for strategic thinking', *Sloan Management Review*, 36(2), 1995, 25–39.

11

Macroenvironmental (STEEP/PEST) analysis

Description and purpose

This chapter focuses on the social, technological, economic, ecological and political/legal (STEEP) aspects of the environment that can affect the competitiveness of industries and companies (also sometimes referred to as political, economic, social and technological (PEST) analysis). These factors are generally considered to be beyond the direct influence of an individual company.

For the purposes of this chapter, and for ease of understanding, we will refer to this technique as STEEP, although you can simplify the technique to PEST factors.

Although many organisations recognise the importance of the environment, all too often this analysis ends up making a small or minimal contribution to strategy analysis and formulation. This can be because the organisation views the environment as being too uncertain to do anything about, or because many environmental factors have delayed or indirect effects on the organisation and therefore often escape the notice of managers who are more concerned with day-to-day operations.

Analysts commonly segment the environment into three distinct levels: the general environment, the operating environment and the internal environment.

Figure 11.1 illustrates the relationship of these levels with each other and the organisation. This book as a whole provides techniques that allow you to understand things happening at all three levels.

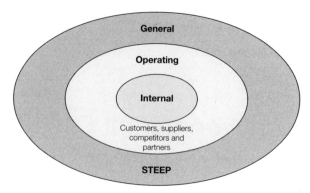

Figure 11.1 The three levels of the environment

Managers must be aware of these environmental levels, know what factors they include, and try to understand how each factor and the relationships among the factors affect organisational performance. The STEEP technique described in this chapter will especially help you to understand the general environmental level.

The general environment is broad in scope and has long-term implications for the organisation and its strategies. These implications are usually understood to be beyond the direct influence of an organisation – for example, the role of government and government legislation on an industry.

The general environment is broken down into sub-categories or segments. One effective segmentation is known as the STEEP categorisation scheme. As described earlier, it also comes under different names, including ones such as PEST, PESTLE, SEPTember, STEEPLES and so on. More important than which of these schemes is chosen, is to recognise that the primary purpose of these segments or subcategories is to avoid overlooking major aspects of the general environment in your overall analysis.

Table 11.1 shows several key variables that would be present under each individual STEEP factor as identified in Figure 11.2. The STEEP sectors are not mutually exclusive – the lines between the categories remain fluid. Issues, events or stakeholders can actually traverse several sectors at once.

Environmental conditions affect the entire strategic management process. Organisations do not operate in a vacuum, and a key to effective strategic management is to make decisions that will enable actions to correspond positively with the context in which those actions will ultimately take place. To some degree, an organisation's internal con-

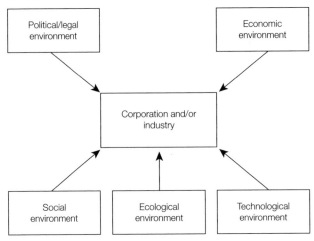

Figure 11.2 The elements of STEEP analysis

ditions, in particular its strengths, weaknesses, resources or capabilities, will determine the action. On the other hand, the action is often largely dictated by external factors. To some extent, any company can shape the environment to its advantage or react in ways that disadvantage it less than its competitors.

Table 11.1 Key STEEP variables

Social	Technological	Ecological	Economic	Political/legal
Ideological characteristics	Patents held	Air and water quality	GDP growth rates	Policies of political parties
Types of union organisations	R&D budgets	Recycling capacity	Exchange reserves	Activism of regulatory agencies
Income gaps among social segments	Number of colleges and universities in a region	Sources of power	Rate of inflation	Presence of property protection laws
Percentage of population in economic and social segments	Pace of technological change	Stage of evolution in the product life cycle	Income distribution levels and bands	Ability to influence political decision making
Value systems for social classes	Presence of technology clusters	Pollution levels	Interest rates	Voting rates and trends

Table 11.1 (continued)

Social	Technological	Ecological	Economic	Political/legal
Cultural background of citizens	Pace of process or product improvements	Substitutability of raw materials	Small business lending levels	Nature of power and decision-making structures
Birth and death rates	Bandwidth capacity	Level of environmental regulation	Balance of payments	Public opinion

Strengths

The key strength of environmental analysis is that it has the explicit task of leading executive thinking beyond current activities and short-term horizons, while still making frequent and sensible links to current and shorter-term activities to retain credibility. To be successful, environmental analysis needs to be linked conceptually and practically to current planning operations – thus it is important to involve key organisational planners in the environmental analysis.

The organisation's process of strategy formulation is considerably weakened unless it has a filtering process that allows it to establish the importance and relevance of external developments. The STEEP technique allows this to happen.

The organisation's decision makers must also develop a structured way of identifying and analysing relevant trends, events and stakeholder expectations in the STEEP environment, including the systematic assessment of environmental change on the company's businesses and action plans. This can be accomplished at an organisation-wide policy level or in a functionally focused way (for example, new products for marketing managers or lobbying strategies for government affairs managers).

An organisation's success or failure can substantially depend on how accurately its decision makers read the environment and respond to it. Therefore, managers must think carefully about who should gather the information and how to structure its flow and use – cross-functional teams of internal specialists can often perform environmental analysis effectively. Having the support and encouragement of top management is an important success factor, as is having appropriate systems established to support the effort.

For environmental analysis to fulfil its purpose, it must 'fit' the organisation's strategy, culture, planning processes and the unique styles of its decision makers.

Successful environmental analysis also needs to be responsive to the information needs of decision makers. As such, these information needs may change over time, and you will need to adjust the environmental analysis in accordance with such changes.

Effective environmental analysis will have a positive effect on competitive performance if proper actions are taken and proper evaluations are made. Timely actions will yield good results over an extended period of time.

Weaknesses

Several empirical studies have shown that the STEEP method of environmental analysis is difficult to do effectively over time. Different types of environmental contexts (for example, dynamic or placid, simple or complex, and continuous or discontinuous) also impact its effectiveness.

Problems in environmental analysis tend to fall within several categories:

■ *Interpretation.* Organisational decision makers often have difficulties in conceptualising or defining what their environment is, making it difficult to interpret the specific kinds of impact the environmental variables will have and the nature of effective responses that the organisation may choose to pursue. Weaknesses in interpreting environmental factors include being able to structure meaningful studies, showing financial impact, synthesising short- and long-term implications, a lack of senior management involvement in the analysis, difficulties in translating potential opportunities into action plans, and appropriating the time and resources required to do accurate analysis.

■ *Inaccuracy and uncertainty.* Problems experienced here include inaccuracies in analytical output and lack of faith in the results due to the presence of too many ambiguities and uncertainties or a combination of both. This can be a result of difficulties in depicting environmental events and trends, and properly characterising uncertainties in meaningful terms as well as difficulties in accurately forecasting the effects of STEEP forces and the social and technological evolution and trends.

■ *Short-term orientation.* Many decision makers dislike spending 'real' money today for speculative results tomorrow and are primarily concerned with short-term matters. Many of the variables in the STEEP segments take numerous years to evolve, frequently far outlasting the analysts and decision makers in the organisations who need to understand them.

■ *Lack of acceptance*. Not accepting the value of environmental analysis can be due to management's lack of understanding of its value, difficulties in encouraging line managers to utilise its outputs, resistance to changing forecasting methods, and presumptions among managers that they are already experts in the implementation and management of this process. Another related issue is the failure to link the STEEP analysis to competitive implications. A key goal of using this technique should always be the identification of competitive implications for the organisation based on the environment analysis.

■ *Misperceptions*. Management's limited scope or invalid perceptions about the environment; for example, thinking in country terms as opposed to global terms.

■ *Diversified businesses*. Human limitations, prior experience and bias affect environmental analysis. This is especially true in multinational environments where home-country biases and attitudes often lead organisations to superimpose their own experiences, views and understanding on variables that do not act in ways suggested or supported by the STEEP factors.

How to do it

The environmental boundaries you define will bind the breadth, depth and forecasting horizon of the analysis. Breadth refers to the topical coverage of the environmental data collected; depth determines the level of detail in the STEEP data being sought and analysed; and forecasting horizons will usually span the short, medium and longer timeframes, as dictated by the relevant organisation's specific environment.

To establish environmental boundaries, examine the organisation's strategic plans with respect to its geographic reach (where it does and does not compete), its product or service scope (segments, categories), its time horizon for returns on fixed resource commitments, technology and innovation, sources of its resources (human, capital, other financial and raw materials), regulatory issues and flexibility. Note that the process will be constrained by the resources available and dedicated to performing the task.

Once the environmental boundaries have been defined, the five STEEP segments can be analysed by addressing the following five-step process:

1   Understand the segment of the environment being analysed.

2   Understand interrelationships between trends.

3   Relate trends to issues.

4   Forecast the future direction of issues.

5   Derive implications.

Step 1: Understand the segment of the environment being analysed

What are the current key events and trends within the segment? Events are important occurrences in the different STEEP domains. Trends are the general tendency for events to occur and the course of those events. For example, within the social segment, you would look to capture trends surrounding work and leisure, consumption and savings, education, travel, religious activities and household work.

What is the evidence supporting the existence of these trends? It is important that data or evidence underlying the existence of trends are captured so as to facilitate continued monitoring and forecasting of the trend's direction and evolution.

How have the trends evolved historically? Like industries, products and organisations, trends have life cycles with identifiable stages – they emerge, develop, peak and decline. You need to identify where a trend is in its life cycle. An understanding of the cycle of trends is critical in identifying their subsequent evolution.

What is the nature and degree of change or turbulence within trends? Trends fluctuate according to their rate of evolution, magnitude and fractionation. Rate of change in a trend requires you to focus on whether the trend is accelerating, decelerating or remaining static in its life cycle. Magnitude looks at the degree of spread associated with a trend and whether it is affecting larger or smaller groups to greater or lesser degrees. Fractionation looks at the relationship of the trend with other trends to see whether the focal trend is impacting or being impacted by other trends.

What kind of impacts do the trends have for the organisation? Conceptually, there are three different kinds of impact that trends may have for the organisation:

■ *Negative impacts.* These are associated with threats to the organisation's ability to achieve its goals. They may also prevent the organisation from acting upon its current strategy, increase its risks associated with moving forward with the existing strategy, increase the level of resources required to implement the strategy, or suggest that a strategy is no longer appropriate.

- *Positive impacts.* These are associated with opportunities for the organisation to achieve its goals. The trends may support or strengthen existing strategies, may increase the likelihood of the organisation being able to implement its planned strategy, or suggest a new opportunity that can be exploited if one or more strategies were changed within the framework of the organisation's existing mission.

- *Neutral or zero impacts.* These may be stabilising or irrelevant forces and may also increase the confidence decision makers have in their strategies.

Step 2: Understand interrelationships between trends

What are the interrelationships between trends? An understanding of the interrelationships requires you to identify the impact between the different STEEP segments and subsegments. Look for areas where trends are suggesting redefinitions or changes from the expected evolutionary path or where they are reinforcing one another.

What are the conflicts between trends? Trends often push in opposite directions and counteract one another. For example, people are becoming more committed to their work at the same time that they are seeking more family time outside of the workplace.

Step 3: Relate trends to issues

Not all trends are of equal importance to an organisation or an industry. Some trends will affect an organisation directly, while others might only have a tangential effect, depending on how they interact with the organisation's strategy and its execution. The astute analyst will identify those trends and combinations of trends that are likely to have the highest impact on the organisation's goals. The most critical ones are defined as 'issues' for the organisation. This is where STEEP and issue analysis (see Chapter 8) find complementarities.

Step 4: Forecast the future direction of issues

Assess the underlying forces. Forecasting the future evolution of a trend or set of trends within an 'issue' requires analysing the driving forces behind the issue. You must be able to distinguish between symptoms and causes – a difficult task, as often the driving forces work against one another and push simultaneously in multiple directions. Once the causes are accurately identified, alternative projections of the issue's evolution can be developed.

Make alternative projections of the issues. To avoid the limitations created by single forecasts, it is useful to develop multiple projections or scenarios. Each of these scenarios will represent a differing view of the future that is developed around clearly identified trends. For example, identify a best case, worst case and neutral case scenario for issue development. Then subject the scenario to a set of questions to test its veracity, such as: what underlying forces are propelling the trends? What is the probability or likelihood that they will continue? How strong is the evidence that its component trends are accurate? Do the interrelationships among the trends make sense? This is where STEEP and scenario analysis (see Chapter 10) find complementarities.

Step 5: Derive implications

Macroenvironmental analysis needs to make a contribution to and serve as an input to the organisation's strategic planning. Implications should be focused on three levels, the following in particular:

1   The structural forces surrounding your industry and any strategic groups within the industry.

2   How they affect your organisation's strategy.

3   How they are expected to affect competitors' strategies.

This assessment should provide the key inputs in determining what future strategies might be.

Life and death of brands

Some of the major brands that currently adorn our homes and offices will face decline and death in the future. Brands, as with every product and service, are affected and/or influenced by a combination of internal (micro) and external (macro) environmental factors. For example, consider the STEEP elements and their influence on brands and the marketplace:

■   *Societal.* Products and the brand names associated with them may become socially unacceptable. People are also generally more observant of newer or more hyped or exciting developments, as opposed to long-standing, comfortable ones. Equally, consumer tastes change and the brand may have lagged behind, thus risking a rapid decline. In other words, the organisation has failed to consider the health of the brand.

▶

■ *Technological*. Technology can create radical change and create great disruptions or distortions in pre-existing markets. The introduction of the Internet has seen the demise of the fax machine and caused great havoc to traditional recording media such as LPs, cassette tapes or compact discs. What products and/or services will nanotechnology change?

■ *Economic*. A recession can have a significant effect on whether current customers can afford to continue purchasing certain types of branded products, particularly luxury or leisure-oriented ones that are generally ascribed to discretionary income categories. Equally, a rise in raw material costs, such as oil, will affect the financial performance of a brand. If there is long-term economic instability, the future of the brand may be in jeopardy. A tip worth keeping in mind is that when looking at economic issues, always look at global economic issues.

■ *Environmental*. Global warming will have an impact on brands in the future and may already be doing so at present in ways yet difficult to pinpoint. Car manufacturers, no matter where they are in the world, will need to consider replacing the current combustion engine, not to mention more deeply consider the life cycles of their products far beyond their useful functional life (cradle to grave thinking). Companies that have invested in alternative power supplies, such as fuel cells, will most likely increase the longevity of their brands.

■ *Political*. If a country is politically unstable, it is likely to be or to become economically unstable. This can have major impact on a brand that is limited to one particular country market. If a brand has regional or international presence, it may be buffered or otherwise protected within those additional markets. The political segment also includes acts of terrorism. The destruction of a Pam Am flight over Lockerbie in Scotland signalled the end of a once dominant international brand.

■ *Legal*. This is often linked to the political situation within a market. Changes in legislation can have serious effects on brand longevity. This can be seen with various tobacco brands that have seen markets reduced due to legislation that restricts or prevents promotion or utilisation of the brands. In some cases, companies have diversified into different product ranges, keeping the ability to leverage or trade on their brand name.

By understanding these influencing factors, an organisation can review its brand position within the marketplace. Moreover, it can attempt to forecast or scenario-plan possible outcomes for its brands, depending on the implication of the trends of the STEEP factors. For example, as mentioned, a tobacco brand facing increasing global promotion and distribution restrictions might seek to diversify into other business areas. It might be able to leverage and re-energise an existing brand name to develop new market opportunities. Marlboro diversified into a range of clothing distributed through its own stores.

Source: Adapted from Groucutt, J., 'The life, death and resuscitation of brands', *Handbook of Business Strategy* (Rockville, MD: Emerald Group, 2006), pp. 101–106.

12

SWOT analysis

Description and purpose

SWOT (strengths, weaknesses, opportunities and threats) analysis is used to evaluate the fit between a company's internal resources and capabilities (that is, its strengths and weaknesses) and external possibilities (that is, opportunities and threats).

A company has a greater degree of practical control over its internal environment – which includes its resources, culture, operating systems and staffing practices, as well as the personal values of the company's managers. These areas are generally subject to the discretionary decision making of the organisation's executives.

A company has lesser control over its external environment – which includes market demand; the degree of market saturation; government policies; economic conditions; social, cultural and ethical developments; technological developments; ecological developments (see Chapter 11 for more about STEEP); and factors making up Porter's five forces (that is, intensity of rivalry, threat of new entrants, threat of substitute products, bargaining power of buyers and bargaining power of suppliers). Refer to Chapter 7 for a detailed discussion of the Five Forces model, also known as industry analysis.

Ken Andrews, regarded as the pioneer of SWOT analysis, in 1971 was one of the first strategy theorists to formally describe the concept of strategic fit between a company's internal environment (its resources and capabilities) and its external environment. He claimed that a SWOT analysis could identify the best way for a company to use its strengths to exploit opportunities and to defend both its strengths and weaknesses against external threats. Figure 12.1 demonstrates the thinking and strategic questioning behind the SWOT technique. Figure 12.2 identifies the SWOT process. In reality, most managers generally only undertake Part A – and may not even do that properly.

SWOT can be applied to many areas of a company, including products, divisions and services. The simplicity and ease of use of this model has made it a very popular technique, particularly for determining a company's

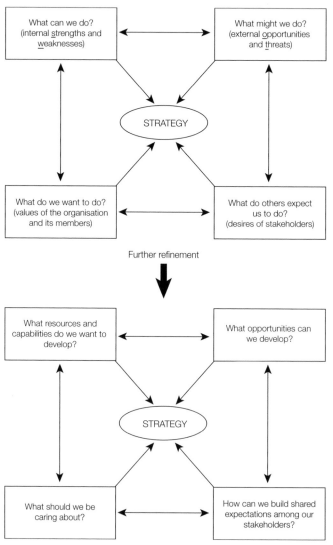

Figure 12.1 The roots of SWOT: key questions that guide strategic choice
Source: Adapted from Clawson, J.G., *Strategic Thinking* (Charlottesville, VA: Darden Graduate, Business School Foundation, 1998), pp. 4–5.

Internal strengths		Internal weaknesses	
1 _____		1 _____	
2 _____		2 _____	
3 _____		3 _____	
4 _____ etc.		4 _____ etc.	
External opportunities		External threats	
1 _____		1 _____	
2 _____		2 _____	
3 _____		3 _____	
4 _____ etc.		4 _____ etc.	

Figure 12.2 Part A – The SWOT technique: identifying, analysing and ranking strategic issues

		Internal factors	
		Strengths	Weaknesses
External factors	Opportunities	Internal strengths matched with external opportunities 1 2 3 4	Internal weaknesses matched with external opportunities 1 2 3 4
	Threats	Internal strengths matched with external threats 1 2 3 4	Internal weaknesses matched with external threats 1 2 3 4

COMPETITIVE ADVANTAGE

Figure 12.2 Part B – Specification of SWOT variables and development of strategy to improve matches

ability to deal with its environment. However, it is also one of the most misused and poorly understood methods of analysis.

SWOT is a common technique for analysing and exploring a company's situation and is often popularly thought of as 'situation analysis'. It guides executives in developing an overall marketplace context for the company.

This analysis consists of both an external and internal component and provides management with an overview and understanding of the forces, trends and characteristics of a particular market. The insights from this analysis are then used to assist managers in making informed choices about what actions to take to maintain a company's comparative advantage (that is, developing its strengths while minimising its weaknesses) and increase its ability to achieve its goals and objectives.

A company analyses its external environment to identify both present and future opportunities and threats that could influence its competitive ability.

A company's external environment consists of two main areas:

- *The operating environment that relates to a particular industry.* Suppliers, competitors, customers, labour and international components.

- *The general environment.* The social, technological, economic, environmental and political/legal (STEEP) components within which the industry and the company are situated.

Environmental analysis can help managers answer the following critical questions:

- What are the competitive forces in our industry, and how strongly will they affect us?
- What factors are affecting competition?
- What are competitors' assumptions about the changing environment?
- What environmental factors are vital to our competitive success?
- Is the industry's environment attractive or unattractive now, and how will it look in the future?

A company's internal operating environment is equally important. To better understand a company's abilities, a manager needs to look at things such as its cost drivers, resources and capabilities.

Overall, a SWOT analysis enables managers to better understand and respond to the factors that can have the greatest impact on a company's performance. These factors are called the company's strategic issues. A strategic issue exists either inside or outside the company and is likely to have a major and long-term impact on the ability of the company to meet its competitive objectives. Strategic issues typically impact across the entire company and require greater resources to effectively address them.

Information derived from a SWOT analysis assists in the identification of strategic issues – such as new technologies, market trends, new competitors and customer satisfaction trends. These in turn require interpretation and translation, as well as the formulation and execution of strategies to address them.

However, a company's internal and external environment changes over time. Vigilant review of strengths, weaknesses, opportunities and threats is required to deal with these ever-changing issues.

Strengths

The SWOT technique is easy to use for organising large amounts of information and for applying a general framework to understand and manage the environment in which a company operates. It can be used to analyse a variety of issues, including individuals, teams, projects, products, services, functional areas (such as accounting, marketing, production and sales), business units and corporations. It works equally well for both profit-making and not-for-profit companies. It can provide insight into why a particular company has been successful or unsuccessful in carrying out its strategy.

Compared with other techniques, it does not require a great deal of external information, financial resources or IT capabilities. It provides an effective framework for identifying the critical issues when dealing with complex situations in a short amount of time.

It enables managers to focus on the issues that have the most impact on the company and those which can be effectively dealt with by their capabilities and resources. It also provides a guide for managers to analyse the options available to them in responding to their competitive environments and assists in evaluating their core capabilities, competencies and resources.

It can be effective for team building when different areas of the business, such as marketing, production and finance, undertake a SWOT together. Managers, for example, can review the strengths, weaknesses, opportunities and threats closest to their specialties and alert colleagues from other departments and senior executives to the issues they see as critical to the SWOT.

The process of collecting, interpreting and organising the many sources of information onto the SWOT grid (see Figure 12.2) also provides an excellent base from which to guide further strategic analysis.

Weaknesses

The SWOT technique masks a great deal of complexity. The primary concern for managers is the collection and interpretation of what can be a large amount of information concerning environmental factors and then deciding what to do in response to it. Interpretation of the information is likely to differ between individual managers – for example, one manager may see the loosening of government-imposed trade barriers between nations as a market expansion opportunity, whereas another may see it as a threat due to competition that might ensue. This far too easily confused set of opportunities and threats is a commonly experienced problem.

Only broadly generalised recommendations are typically offered from a SWOT analysis, such as moving the company away from threats, matching the company's strengths with opportunities, or defending against the weaknesses through divestment or investment. It is also limited in its ability to help a company identify specific actions to follow. It provides little guidance relative to strategy execution.

The data used tend to be qualitative rather than quantitative – and focus on delivering reactive rather than proactive strategies. Weaknesses tend to be more broadly identified, while strengths tend to be more narrowly defined. In fact, managers are frequently too optimistic in their assessment of a company's strengths and opportunities versus their weaknesses and threats. Weaknesses are often ignored entirely, especially in situations where the SWOT is performed under conditions of political resource scarcity or infighting.

It often fails because of managers' blind spots regarding the company's capabilities.[1] Due to the subjective nature of this process, it may be appropriate for an outsider to assist managers with the SWOT to ensure biases are kept at a minimum. Otherwise, the results of your SWOT analysis will not be used to inform and drive strategy but will be viewed as a 'Substantial Waste of Time', an outcome you should be careful to avoid!

How to do it

The process for gathering and interpreting information in a SWOT analysis should be an interrelated and reinforcing process of consultation and verification with executives, functional experts and team members. Additionally, acquiring and utilising the perceptions of customers can also be highly illuminating in this process.

Step 1: List and evaluate SWOT elements

The first step involves listing and evaluating the company's strengths, weaknesses, opportunities and threats:

■ *Strengths* are those factors that make a company more competitive than its rivals. It is where the company has an advantage over or superior assets to the competition. A strength is meaningful only when it is useful to satisfy an existing or prospective customer need. When this is the case, that strength becomes a capability. Strengths are, in effect, capabilities and resources that the company can use effectively to achieve its performance objectives. When addressing strengths, it is important to keep to the facts and not get caught up in cultural biases or blind spots.

■ *Weaknesses* are limitations, faults or defects within the company that can prevent it from achieving its objectives. It is when the company performs poorly or has inferior capabilities or resources to the competition. While some weaknesses may be relatively harmless, those that relate to specific existing or future customer needs should be minimised if possible. Again, you need to be mindful of blind spots.

■ *Opportunities* relate to any favourable current or prospective situation in the external environment, such as a trend, change or overlooked need that supports a product or service and permits the company to enhance its competitive position.

■ *Threats* include any unfavourable situation, trend or impending change in the external environment that currently or potentially damages or threatens the company's ability to compete.

You may want to refer to such techniques as the value chain, Porter's Five Forces or STEEP to ensure that you are identifying a broad range of strengths, weaknesses, opportunities and threats both for now and in the future.

Although many published SWOT analyses stop at the end of this step, all that you have really done is produce four separate lists of factors. We describe this interim output as 'four bunches of bullet points' that have undergone only minimal thought or transformation. This is not analysis in any professional sense and should never be allowed to be a substitute for constructive analysis. The astute analyst will recognise this step is only a starting point and will proceed with the following steps.

Step 2: Analyse and rank strategic factors

This step of the SWOT analysis will look similar to Part A of Figure 12.2 – a ranked list (by aspects such as importance or magnitude) of factors classified as internal strengths and weaknesses and external opportunities and threats. It is important to widely share criteria for the ranking so that the company can better understand the basis upon which they are prioritised. Involving managers and outside experts, as well as customers or other objective parties, is important to producing useful and valid outputs in this step. You may want to create a template along the lines shown in Table 12.1.

Table 12.1 A SWOT template

SWOT Internal strengths	SCORE 1	2	3	4	5
(a)					
(b)					
(c)					
(d)					
Internal weaknesses	1	2	3	4	5
(a)					
(b)					
(c)					

Unfortunately, this is where most managers often stop, believing that the ranking itself is the analytical process of the SWOT analysis. However, strategies for competitive advantage still have to be developed, and this may require further work to identify clearly the causal factors leading to the particular strengths or weaknesses of the organisation.

Step 3: Identify strategic fit and develop a strategy to improve matches

The next step is to identify the company's strategies and strategic fit in light of its internal capabilities and external environment. The resulting fit or misfit should indicate the degree of strategic change the company must make.

In a general sense, you should attempt to develop and recommend strategies that convert important weaknesses into strengths and important threats into opportunities. Finding new markets for a firm's products or services is often a useful conversion strategy. Conversion strategies often require the investment of additional resources, whether in the form of plant, property, equipment, funds or human.

You should also consider strategies that minimise those weaknesses or avoid the threats that cannot be converted. One strategy is to become a niche player within the larger industry. Another one is to reposition the company's products or services.

Four scenarios will become evident as you fill in the quadrants in Part B of Figure 12.2 – these will help to determine the existing strategic fit and develop effective strategies to respond to forecasted environmental issues.

To properly determine the strategic fit, try to visualise the company's performance in the future. What will it be if no changes are made to its strategy and its internal and external environments do not change? Also evaluate alternative strategies to find one that provides a competitive advantage for the company. However, while no strategy may become evident that produces a competitive advantage, a SWOT analysis, at a minimum, will help a company to evaluate current and alternative strategies.

Quadrant 1: Internal strengths matched with external opportunities

This is the ideal as it represents the tightest fit between the company's resources and its external competitive opportunities. The strategy would be to protect internal strengths by either finding the combination of resources needed to achieve competitive advantage or augmenting resources to enhance competitive advantage. Explore opportunities to leverage strengths to bolster weaknesses in other areas (most notably those in Quadrant 2).

Quadrant 2: Internal weaknesses relative to external opportunities

The strategy in this quadrant is to choose the optimal trade-off between investing to turn the weaknesses into strengths, outsourcing a weakness where the company does not have a competitive advantage, or allowing rivals to address this particular area.

Quadrant 3: Internal strengths matched with external threats

A strategic option here could be to transform external threats into opportunities by changing, altering or reconfiguring company resources.

Alternatively, choose to maintain a defensive strategy in order to focus on more promising opportunities in other quadrants.

Quadrant 4: Internal weaknesses relative to external threats

This quadrant needs to be carefully addressed and monitored. If the company's survival is at stake as a result of the issues in this quadrant, a proactive strategy may be the only option. If the strategic issues are secondary, a possible option may be to divest in order to focus on other more promising opportunities in other quadrants. It is important, however, to avoid rushing an issue out of this quadrant. Rather, consider the potential it has to provide a significant strategic option to the company or to support more profitable activities in other quadrants. Blind spot analysis to reduce any cultural or thinking biases may be a useful technique for this quadrant.

This step would look as shown in Table 12.2.

Once a strategy is decided on, constantly monitor and analyse current strategies and devise new ones to address developing issues. Consider this approach as a sweep over the environmental radar screen to monitor the movement of identified blips and to benefit from the early warning capabilities afforded by the SWOT technique.

Table 12.2 The SWOT matrix

Internal *External*	*Strengths*	*Weaknesses*
Opportunities	**SO strategies:** Strategies that leverage internal strengths matched with external opportunities	**WO strategies:** Strategies that leverage external opportunities to overcome or minimise internal weaknesses
Threats	**ST strategies:** Strategies that leverage your internal strengths to avoid external threats	**WT strategies:** Strategies that minimise your internal weaknesses and avoid external threats

Remember, a separate SWOT analysis is required for each business, product, service or market. One SWOT analysis cannot be all things to all issues. These analyses should be conducted regularly to address the dynamic environment in which we all operate.

There are three guidance points to keep in mind when undertaking a SWOT analysis:

■ extremely long lists indicate that the screening criteria used to separate information from the strategic issues is too broad

■ the absence of weighting factors indicates a lack of prioritisation

■ short and ambiguously phrased descriptions within each SWOT factor can indicate that the strategic implications have not been considered.

Cannondale Bicycle Corporation

Headquartered in Bethel, Connecticut, Cannondale Bicycle Corporation (Cannondale) designs, develops and produces bicycles at its factory in Bedford, Pennsylvania. The company operates subsidiaries in Holland, Japan and Australia and is owned by Pegasus Partners II, LP, a private equity investment firm based in Greenwich, Connecticut. Its mission is to create innovative, quality products that inspire cyclists around the world. Even though it is helped by its three-plus decade track record, Cannondale faces an intense and dynamic global industry environment. The SWOT analysis shown in Table 12.3 presents an integrative view of how its external environment combines with its resources and capabilities (the internal factors) to provide for actionable strategies that can assist the company to achieve its mission.

Table 12.3 SWOT matrix for Cannondale Bicycle Corporation

Internal / External	STRENGTHS (S)	WEAKNESSES (W)
Internal / External	1 Brand recognition 2 Full-line provider across entire value chain 3 Scope of retail channels (high-end bike shops) 4 Design and engineering prowess 5 Commitment and dedication of employees	1 Mixed results in diversification efforts 2 High cost of engineering and design talent 3 Less experience with carbon frame production 4 Component range low in market share 5 Lack of recognition in apparel markets
OPPORTUNITIES (O) 1. Co-production of carbon frames in Asia 2. Competitive road and mountain bike teams on three continents seek sponsors	SO strategies 1 Partner with TopKey for carbon frame production (S2, S4, O1, O3) 2 Inexpensively acquire Asian shoe producer (S1, S3, O3, O5)	WO strategies 1 Tap into waiting sources of investor capital (W1, W3, W5, O3, O5) 2 Expand retail partner network in Asia (W5, O2, O3)

▶

OPPORTUNITIES (O)	SO strategies	WO strategies
3 Consolidation in industry favours full-line operators and wide retail availability 4 Unique designs being favoured 5 Expansion into cycling-related apparel where demand is rising	3 Use forward contracts and hedging for carbon fibre supply (S2, O1) 4 Leverage Sugoi into carbon fibre shoes, jerseys and bibs (S1, S3, S5, O4, O5)	3 Sponsor new Asian professional continental team (W5, O2, O5)
THREATS (T)	ST strategies	WT strategies
1 Professional cycling under siege 2 Carbon fibre shortages, high cost of supply 3 Boutique shops attacking high end of market 4 Key new components (drive-train) may require design rethinks 5 Large investments being made into commodity-end (mass market) of business	1 Sponsor club teams in key regions (T1, T5, S1, S5) 2 Rapid prototype components based on relationships developed in testing process (S2, S4, S5, T3, T4) 3 Enhance relationships with full range component suppliers such as Shimano, SRAM and Campagnolo (S2, S4, T4, T5)	1 Emphasise aluminum frames and components (W2, W3, T2, T4) 2 Divest certain component design and production facilities (W1, W4, T3, T4) 3 Restructure distribution locations to more quickly supply high demand regions (W5, T3, T5)

Note: The numbers following each strategy reflect the interrelationship between identified factors in the development of a particular strategy.

Endnote

1 See Chapter 10 in the authors' book *Strategic and Competitive Analysis: Methods and Techniques for Analyzing Business Competition* (Upper Saddle River, NJ: Prentice Hall, 2003) for a detailed treatment of blind spot analysis.

13

Value chain analysis

Description and purpose

Value chain analysis (VCA) is used to identify a company's potential sources of economic advantage and to achieve an optimal allocation of resources. This is done by reviewing its internal core competencies in light of its external environment. A company's value chain is part of a larger industry value system and includes the value creating activities of all of the industry participants – from raw materials suppliers through to the final consumer. VCA separates the company's processes into strategically relevant value creating activities. This analysis provides rich insights into industry profit and assists in identifying strategies needed to generate competitive advantage.

The unique strength of VCA is that it can be used to help companies bridge the strategic gaps between their capabilities and opportunities and threats in their competitive environments. Hence, the two main purposes of VCA are to identify opportunities to secure cost advantages and create product/service attribute differentiation.

The goal of VCA is to help identify strategies that allow your organisation to create customer value in excess of the costs of delivering that value – the source of a company's profit. Cost advantages can be achieved by reconfiguring the entire value chain to lessen overall costs or the costs of any of the key activities along the chain. Likewise, differentiation can be achieved through value chain reconfiguration or by delivering innovative ways of generating higher value from a particular activity.

Michael Porter popularised the value chain concept in his 1985 book, *Competitive Advantage* (see Figure 13.1).

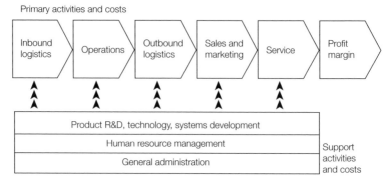

Figure 13.1 The value chain
Source: Adapted from Porter, M.E., *Competitive Advantage* (New York: The Free Press, 1985).

Porter classifies all of these activities into two main categories:

1 Primary activities:

- *inbound logistics* – activities such as inventory warehousing and handling

- *operations* – transformation of inputs into the final product or service

- *outbound logistics* – distribution-oriented activities

- *marketing and sales* – marketing communications, pricing and channel management

- *service* – post-sale support activities.

2 Support activities:

- *technology development* – engineering, R&D and information technology

- *human resource development* – recruitment, incentive systems, motivation, training, promotion and industrial relations

- *company infrastructure* – administrative support activities such as accounting, legal, planning and all forms of stakeholder relations (government and public affairs, community investment and investor relations).

The price charged to the company's customers, less the costs of all of these activities, determines the company's profit. Obviously, you should be looking to see if your organisation is deriving its highest potential margin from the activities it chooses to participate in.

All of the suppliers of the company's inputs as well as forward channel purchasers of the company's products or services will also have their own value
chains composed of their primary and support activities. Collectively, all of
these value chains comprise the industry value system shown in Figure 13.2.

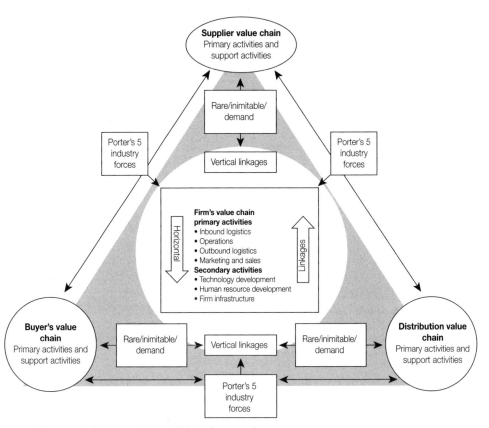

Figure 13.2 Value chains within industry value systems

The totality of activities in the industry's entire value system determines the
total customer value created. It is the customers, in deciding the prices they
are willing to pay for the products/services produced by the industry, who
ultimately determine the margins earned by all of the participants in the
industry value system. The share of industry profit earned by each partici-
pant is determined by Porter's Five Forces, which shape the industry's
structure (see Chapter 7).

VCA is used to determine the current power of the company and suggest
how it can increase that power to gain a higher share of industry profit. The

following list ranks the various types of value chain links in order of their increasing capability to generate competitive advantage:

- *Separate individual activities within the company's value chain.* For example, being an industry leader in inbound logistics.

- *Interlinked primary activities in the company's value chain.* For example, increasing quality inspection, which reduces rework, scrap and customer returns, and increases customer value

- *Interlinked secondary activities in the company's value chain.* For example, an organisational structure that fosters learning in all of the relevant activity areas of the company

- *Vertical links within the industry value system.* For example, developing close relationships with suppliers and customers to co-develop low cost or differentiated strategies for mutual but usually disproportionate benefit that is dependent on each party's bargaining strength in the larger value system

VCA will pinpoint opportunities to radically reconfigure industry value systems by eliminating or bypassing entire value chains or major activities within an industry's value system. A well-known example of this is Amazon's innovative use of technology and relationship management to bypass the traditional book retailer channel through developing close ties with publishing houses and selling solely over the Internet.

There are also many different secondary applications or subsets of VCA used in the pursuit of competitive strategy. These include:

- *Competitor analysis.* Analysing competitors' cost structures, business models and sources of differentiation are intrinsic to crafting strategy.

- *Customer value analysis.* Incorporating the common thread of customer value creating activities into the strategy formulation process provides insight that keeps the analysis relevant to this lowest common denominator of profit.

- *Strategic cost management.* Expanding cost management from the traditional approaches of universal cost containment and reduction across the company (to incorporate the unique cost drivers for each value activity) allows for better management of costs. For example, VCA allows the company to identify and then exploit vertical links with suppliers and customers.

- *Integration.* VCA helps companies invest wisely in vertical or horizontal integration strategies or, conversely, to divest, by understanding the impact of the company's value chain and its strategic position in the industry's value system.

▪ *Supply chain management.* Determining the bargaining power of suppliers as well as recognising their position in the same industry value system potentially generates opportunities for mutually beneficial cooperation.

▪ *Strategic outsourcing.* This requires knowledge of the core competencies that can be provided by VCA. With a grasp of the company's core competencies and the relative importance of various activities in the value chain, strategic outsourcing decisions can be made that reduce costs or improve differentiation and flexibility without harming the company's competitive advantage.

▪ *Acquisition, mergers, alliances or joint ventures.* Synergy or strategic fit can be advantageously framed by VCA. Target companies can be selected on the basis of how the acquisition would enhance the company's strength in the industry's value system.

▪ *Organisational structure.* Drawing the boundaries of organisational units based on discrete value creating activities and the vertical links of the value chain will put the company more in tune with the sources of its competitive advantage.

Porter recommended VCA to encourage companies to exploit the often ignored potential vertical synergies that exist between a company's business units and other participants in the industry value system. The logic of VCA is that most sources of competitive advantage lie in these (often intangible) synergies.

Strengths

From the company's perspective, VCA is a useful tool for understanding its strengths and weaknesses. From an industry perspective, VCA provides a helpful understanding of its competitive position relative to key customers and suppliers. VCA also provides a good understanding of the nature and sustainability of the company's resources and capabilities and what new resources and capabilities it might require to be competitive in the future. For those individuals who are doing a SWOT analysis as part of their insight development process, the VCA will provide a much better real-world sense of what is really a strength or a weakness (see Chapter 12).

VCA encourages the company to comprehensively review all of the value creating activities that deliver value to the customer. It is also more inclusive of the complex economic cost drivers that affect customer value, such as structural drivers (for example, scale, scope, experience, technology and complexity) and executional drivers (for example, management style, total quality management, plant layout, capacity utilisation, product configuration, vertical links with suppliers and customers).

As we can see, VCA builds a holistic cost/value analysis that more closely models economic reality because of its external customer and industry focus. It can help to generate ideas about new revenue-side and cost-based pathways for adding value.

If your company has adopted activity-based accounting (ABA), the process of VCA will be easier, as ABA eliminates many of the distortions of traditional management accounting. In fact, activity-based management (ABM shares many similarities with VCA) works particularly well for those companies that already employ activity-based costing (ABC), competitor benchmarking, Six Sigma or similar management accounting or statistical control processes. Combined and updated with these sources of data, VCA can generate some of the best, empirically based insights for understanding exactly where margin is augmented or deteriorated.

Weaknesses

Despite the strengths of VCA, its usefulness is being challenged by the radical changes that information technologies have wrought. A growing school of management thought asserts that traditional value chains oriented around vertical linkages cannot constantly reinvent value at the speed required for successful strategy.

Traditional VCA was developed for understanding physical assets and flows. It may not be as appropriate to employ for competition based around intellectual assets and services. Having stated that, there are newer conceptual developments happening that increasingly allow for modification of the traditional VCA for evolving or newer modes of competitiveness including value net analysis, value grid analysis, value migration, value constellation analysis, value stream mapping, value shop analysis, service value chains and so on.

Managing value chains in an information communication and technology environment requires the inclusion of economic realities that are not explicitly addressed by Porter's VCA model. VCA treats information as a supporting element in the company's strategy – at best it is only part of a secondary activity. Recently evolved models such as the virtual value chain and value web management treat information as a separate and distinct value creating factor that must be managed separately but together with the enduring physical value chain.

Porter has also been criticised for being too simplistic because many of his qualitative prescriptions are difficult to implement quantitatively – the most prominent shortcoming being that they require significant amounts of resources. Effective VCA requires a large investment in benchmarking, customer research, competitive analysis and industry structure analysis, often using data that are either not freely or easily available. Conducting VCA might be straightforward in theory, but it is relatively difficult and time-consuming to apply for maximum and relevant effect.

Furthermore, most of a company's internal accounting data are incompatible with the analytical dimensions of VCA for several reasons. Traditional management accounting systems rarely, if ever:

■ collect data around value creating activities – instead, they collect data around product/service and period costs

■ collect period costs by product or service, making it difficult to accurately assign overhead costs to value creating processes

■ collect data around cost drivers – departmental budgets will rarely be an accurate source for determining the actual cost of value creating activities

■ enable transfer prices and arbitrary cost allocation of traditional management accounting systems to appropriately encompass the synergies created by horizontal links in the company's value chain or the vertical links in the industry's value system.

How to do it

Conducting a successful VCA requires judgement, attention to detail, competitive knowledge and quantitative analysis. Understanding the company's industry structure and, more importantly, aligning this knowledge with the company's capabilities, are intrinsic to crafting successful strategies.

The VCA process begins with an internal analysis of the company's value chain followed by an external competitive analysis of the industry value system. It concludes by integrating these two analyses to identify and create a strategy that can potentially sustain competitive advantage.

Step 1: Define the company's strategic business units

The first level of review draws boundaries around the various segments of the business. This is necessary because the different segments of the business will have different sources of competitive advantage that require different strategies.

Usually, the company's organisational structure or accounting system will not classify business units in a manner consistent with business unit operations. You must frequently divorce yourself from the usual classifications, such as departments and functions or cost, revenue and investment centres. This leaves you with two conflicting criteria to define your business units either by:

- autonomy (where managerial decisions about one business unit will have little or no impact on the other business unit)
- their ability to support VCA (shared links within the company and between value chains in the value system).

Where the two criteria conflict, it is probably best to choose the latter, as a key purpose of VCA is to leverage shared linkages – a high potential source of competitive advantage.

Step 2: Identify the company's critical value creating activities

For companies that haven't adopted ABA, Porter offers several distinctions that define value creating activities. They are those that:

- have different economic structures
- contribute to a large or growing percentage of total costs
- contribute to or stand a high probability of contributing to product/service differentiation.

Tables 13.1 and 13.2 might provide suggestions of what to look for.

Table 13.1 Assessing the primary activities in the value chain

Inbound logistics

- What type of inventory control system is there? How well does it work?
- How are raw materials handled and warehoused? How efficiently?
- How is material received? From whom? Where is it acquired?

Operations

Areas to be reviewed include machining, testing, packaging, equipment maintenance and so on, with questions such as:

- How productive and efficient is our equipment compared to our competitors?

- What type of plant layout is used? How efficient is it?

- Are production control systems in place to control quality and reduce costs? How efficient and effective are they in doing so?

- Are we using the appropriate level of automation in our production processes? Are employees properly trained to use it? Is it upgradeable?

Outbound logistics

- Are finished products warehoused efficiently? How much waste do we experience?

- How do we manage order processing? What percentage is automated?

- Are finished products efficiently delivered to customers? Are our delivery operations appropriate and effective?

- Are finished products delivered in a timely fashion to customers?

Marketing and sales

- Is marketing research effectively used to identify customer segments and needs?

- Are sales promotions and advertising innovative?

- Have alternative distribution channels been evaluated? How do we select and manage our distribution channels?

- How competent is the sales force operation? Is its level of motivation as high as it can be? Are they perceived to be helpful to customers, both current and potential?

- Does our organisation present an image of quality to our customers? Does our organisation have a favourable reputation?

- How brand-loyal are our customers and our competitors' customers? Does our customer brand loyalty need improvement?

- Do we dominate the various market segments we're in?

Customer service

- How well do we solicit customer input for product improvements?

- How promptly and effectively are customer complaints handled?

- Are our product warranty and guarantee policies appropriate?

- How effectively do we train employees in customer education and service issues?

■ How well do we handle installation?

■ How well do we provide replacement parts and repair services?

Source: Adapted from Coulter, M.K., *Strategic Management in Action*, 2nd edn (Upper Saddle River, NJ: Prentice Hall, 2002), p. 133.

Table 13.2 Assessing the support activities in the value chain

Procurement

■ Have we developed alternative suppliers for all our needed resources?

■ Are resources procured in a timely fashion? At lowest possible cost? At acceptable quality levels?

■ Is purchasing centralised or decentralised? Which would be most effective and efficient?

■ How efficient and effective are our procedures for procuring large capital expenditure resources such as plants, machinery and buildings?

■ Are criteria in place for deciding on lease versus purchase decisions?

■ Have we established sound long-term relationships with reliable suppliers?

Technological development

■ How successful have our research and development activities been in product and process innovations?

■ Is the relationship between R&D employees and other departments strong and reliable? Do they work seamlessly with one another?

■ Have technology development activities been able to meet criteria deadlines?

■ What is the quality of our organisation's laboratories and other research facilities?

■ Have we taken advantage of office automation and telecommunications technologies?

■ Does our organisational culture encourage creativity and innovation?

Human resource management

■ How effective are our procedures for recruiting, selecting, orienting and training employees?

■ Are there appropriate employee promotion policies in place, and are they used effectively?

■ How appropriate are reward systems for motivating and challenging employees?

■ Do we have a work environment that minimises absenteeism and keeps turnover at reasonable levels?

■ Are union–organisation relations (if applicable) acceptable?

■ Do managers and technical personnel actively participate in professional
  organizations?

■ Are employees empowered with decision-making capabilities as required?

■ Are levels of employee motivation, job commitment and job satisfaction
  acceptable?

Company infrastructure

■ Is our organisation able to identify potential external opportunities or threats?
  Do we have an early warning system?

■ Does our strategic planning system facilitate and enhance the
  accomplishment of organisational goals?

■ Can we obtain relatively low cost funds for capital expenditures and working
  capital?

■ Does our information system support strategic and operational decision
  making? Does our information system provide timely and accurate information
  on general environmental trends and competitive conditions?

■ Do our communication processes facilitate fast and transparent message
  sharing with key stakeholders, both inside and outside the organisation?

■ Do we have good relationships with all our stakeholders including public
  policy makers, interest groups and so on?

■ Do we have a good public image of being a responsible corporate citizen?

Source: Adapted from Coulter, M.K. *Strategic Management in Action*, 2nd edn (Upper Saddle
River, NJ: Prentice Hall, 2002), p. 134.

Step 3: Conduct an internal cost analysis

An internal cost analysis is composed of the following:

1 *Assign costs to each critical value creating activity identified in Step 2.* It is
  recommended that a full costing or a product life cycle costing
  approach be used that incorporates full capacity utilisation.

2 *Find the cost drivers for each critical value creating activity that is driven by
  more than one major cost category.* Structural cost drivers are long term
  in nature and affect the economic cost structure of the company's
  products and services. (Consider scale, scope, learning curves,
  technology and complexity.) Executional cost drivers are more
  operational in nature. (Consider management style, total quality
  management, plant layout, capacity utilisation, product configuration,
  and vertical links with suppliers and customers.)

3 *Diagnose the company's current strategy for areas of potential low cost
  advantage.* Search for horizontal links in the company's value chain in

the form of interlinked value creating activities that reduce costs by virtue of their symbiosis. This is the time to explore opportunities for cost management. It is important to focus externally to compare the company's cost structure to its competition through benchmarking and associated practice comparisons. Business process design and re-engineering approaches can then be utilised to secure any potential low cost advantages.

Step 4: Conduct an internal differentiation analysis

Similar to the internal cost analysis, the internal differentiation analysis starts with identifying the company's value creating activities and cost drivers. Next, you link your customer and competitive knowledge with the appropriate strategy through the following steps:

1 *Conduct customer research to determine a precise definition of customer value.* Helpful ways to secure this knowledge are to engage in a dialogue with customers and analyse the customer's own value chain to gain insights into how your company's products and services may provide additional value to them.

2 *Identify strategies that can differentiate your company's products and services.* This could include product or service attributes, channel management, customer support, pre- and post-sale support, branding and price. Based on the company's core competencies, choose the best differentiation strategy to achieve competitive advantage by offering a product or service that is rare, in demand and difficult for competitors to imitate.

Step 5: Map the industry profit pool

(i) Define the parameters of the industry profit pool

The parameters of the industry profit pool are dependent on the value chain processes that affect the company's current and future ability to earn profit. It is helpful to assume the perspective of the company, competitors and customers. Include all of the relevant value creating activities, starting with the purchase of raw material inputs and ending with the total cost of ownership to the final consumer. Note, the final consumer may not be your company's purchasers.

(ii) Estimate the total size of the industry profit pool

Employ several different estimation methodologies to gauge the total size of the profit pool, for example by companies, products, channels or regions. Usually, accounting profit will suffice for profit. However, when mapping the profit pool of an industry with international participants, economic value added (EVA) can be used because it eliminates many of the distortions caused by various national generally accepted accounting principles (GAAP) regimes. Some sources of information for these estimates are analyst reports, financial statements, security commission reports and by engaging industry experts.

(iii) Estimate the distribution of the profit pool

A good starting point is to use your company's profit structure by activity (that is, Steps 1 to 4) in the external analysis of rival companies in the industry. Following are a few general rules for this stage:

■ Use your knowledge of the underlying economics of your own company to outline each activity's profit. Take care to segregate allocated costs. This information can be used as a relative gauge to estimate the activity profits of rival companies in the industry.

■ Sources of competitive information include financial statements, analyst reports, security exchange commission filings, trade journals, the business press, industry associations and government regulators.

■ A helpful hint is to use the market value or replacement costs of assets that support value creating activities and the full costing approach under full capacity for costing the same value creating activities.

■ Use the 80/20 rule – this suggests that 20 per cent of the industry's companies will generate 80 per cent of the industry profit; therefore, concentrate on the largest companies first.

■ The level of analytical detail will depend on the degree of vertical integration present in the industry. Start with the focused companies first and then estimate the relevant activity profits of diversified companies by adjusting your knowledge of your own company's economics and that of the focused companies in the industry. Next, include the smaller companies (the 80 per cent responsible for 20 per cent of industry profit), based on sampling.

■ For accuracy, total the activity profits determined in this step and compare them to the total industry profit pool determined in Step 5(ii) earlier. If the two estimates are wildly divergent, change the assumptions and tweak the methodology through iteration until the two estimates are reasonably similar.

A graphical representation of an industry profit pool should look similar to Figure 13.3. The results could be surprising in that the activities that command the largest industry revenue share may receive a disproportionately low share of industry profits.

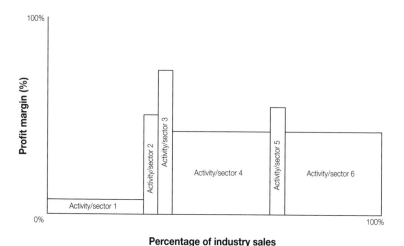

Figure 13.3 Stylistic industry profit pool graphic

Step 6: Vertical linkage analysis

The opportunities to achieve cost and differentiation advantages within the company's value chain were reviewed in Steps 1 to 4. Step 5 allowed you to determine whether the company is strategically positioned in the shallow or deep end of the industry's profit pool. Vertical linkage analysis allows you to seek out opportunities to exploit the most important sources of competitive advantage in the industry's value system. You can combine your intimate knowledge of the company's economic structure, customer value, and external competitive analysis to determine how to reposition the company into the deep end of the industry profit pool – and keep it there.

The methodology to accomplish this is the crux of vertical linkage analysis. This is also the most difficult stage because many of the vertical linkages in the industry's value chain are less tangible and extremely difficult to discover. Nevertheless, it is because of this difficulty that VCA often offers a direct route to competitive advantage. The methodology consists of the following stages:

1   Use Porter's Five Forces model to determine the industry's economic structure (see Chapter 7).

2   Determine the cost drivers and core competencies driving the low cost or differentiation for each of the value creating activities of competitors.

3   Evaluate the company's core competencies – those capabilities, skills and technologies that create low cost or differentiated customer value. Usually, core competencies are acquired through collective learning and relationships. Identify any opportunities to surpass competing customer offerings by securing missing competencies or supplementing existing competencies needed to successfully craft, maintain and strengthen a low cost or differentiation strategy.

4   Based on the relative bargaining strength of other value chains in the value system, determine opportunities to acquire or strengthen the required competencies through vertical linkages with suppliers, channels or buyers in the value system.

5   Avoid the temptation to settle for a mixed strategy – part differentiation and part low cost. This is the easy way, but it will not generate competitive advantage for the average company; rather, it will leave a company wading aimlessly in the shallow end of the industry profit pool. A growing body of academic work, validated by practice, asserts that crafting successful strategy is valuable because of the often painful trade-offs it forces executives to make. Mixed strategies offer a chance of success only for companies that are pushing the frontier of production possibilities or for those that have a truly integrated global strategy.

6   Identify any potential opportunities for competitive advantage in the vertical linkages between the company's value chain and the value chains of suppliers, channels and customers. By co-opting or cooperating with other value chains in the industry's value system, the company can often craft a low cost or differentiated strategy that is impossible for competitors to replicate. Complex and less or intangible vertical linkages offer the most impenetrable combinations of rarity, demand and inimitability – the triad underlying competitive advantage.

Step 7: Iteration

Repeat Steps 1 to 6 periodically by making VCA a central component of your company's competitive intelligence and strategy development system in order to proactively manage evolutionary and revolutionary industry change.

IKEA

Sweden's IKEA presents an excellent example of how companies can use the concept of VCA to reconfigure industry value chains to their benefit. VCA played a prominent role in IKEA's growth from a small, domestic, mail-order furniture company into a multinational chain of more than 260 stores in more than 37 countries with 2007 revenues of 20.6 million euros and a global customer base of over 580 million. More importantly, IKEA has profitably managed this growth, as witnessed by an estimated 10 per cent profit margin in a notoriously low margin discount furniture industry. An initial analysis of IKEA's business model would suggest that it was able to achieve this through efficient and effective management of its internal value chain: low cost components, efficient warehousing and customer self-service have allowed it to offer discounts 25–50 per cent below its competitors. IKEA's true source of success goes much deeper than this, however, and can be shown by its skillful management of the industry value system.

IKEA has successfully reconfigured its industry value system by redefining almost every aspect of its industry through leveraging vertical links in its value system. It used many of the individual value chains within its industry value system to increase its power in the furniture industry.

Supplier's value chain

IKEA has 38 factories in 11 countries, mostly in Eastern and Central Europe, and its operations cover every step of production – forestry, sawmilling, board manufacture and furniture production.

However, a major source of IKEA's low cost is derived from extensive outsourcing. IKEA works closely with its suppliers in a cooperative relationship to mutually exploit synergies. Forty-five IKEA trading offices in 31 countries evaluate 1,350 suppliers in 50 countries for low cost and high quality. Furniture designers in the home office in Almhut, Sweden, work two to three years ahead of the current product life cycle to determine which supplier will provide parts. Once accepted, IKEA provides suppliers with economies of scale associated with global markets, technical assistance and leased equipment. Suppliers also receive quality advice from IKEA engineers and have access to a computer database to assist in sourcing raw materials and matching suppliers with each other from the business service department.

Distribution value chain

To manage and support its global network of suppliers, IKEA operates 31 distribution centres in 16 countries. These centres supply goods to IKEA stores and ensure that the route from supplier to customer is as direct, cost-effective and environmentally friendly as possible. Efficient distribution plays a key role in maintaining low prices.

Direct links from every cash register in every store to these warehouses are an integral part of the cost reduction strategy, as they support lean inventory management. They also support customer value by allowing IKEA to tightly integrate supply with demand.

Customer value chain

The cornerstone of IKEA's strategy is to convince customers that it is in their best interests to assume more responsibility in creating value by performing more activities in the industry value system themselves – choosing, ordering, delivering and assembling products in exchange for low cost, high quality products. To encourage this radical redesign of the value system, IKEA employs its core competence – its knowledge of how to make these activities easy, enjoyable and valuable for its customers:

■ IKEA produces more than 191 million catalogues per annum in 56 editions and 27 languages for 34 countries/territories. Each catalogue carries only 30 to 40 per cent of the entire 9,500-item product line, transcending the traditional role of the catalogue as a simple ordering tool. The IKEA website also attracted 450 million visits during the last 12 months worldwide. In effect, the catalogue and the Internet function as a role-playing guide, essentially explaining to the customer what is expected of them in exchange for exceptional discounts on high quality furniture at their local IKEA stores.

■ Shopping at IKEA is designed to be fun. IKEA provides shoppers with many value-creating amenities that increase the value of the shopping experience – strollers, supervised daycare, playgrounds, cafes, restaurants and wheelchairs for the disabled, some of which are free of charge.

■ Shopping at IKEA is easy, quick and productive. The company provides several tools to assist customers in creating their own value in partnership with IKEA. Items such as catalogues, tape measures, pens and paper are provided free of charge. Design ideas are created through IKEA's store displays. Each item in these displays is tagged with only the necessary details – product name, price, available dimensions, materials, colour, care instructions, and order and pickup location. If the chosen merchandise doesn't fit in the customer's vehicle, IKEA will lend a roof rack.

VCA has allowed IKEA to offer its customers what no one else has – a large selection of high quality furniture at low cost. This combination dismisses many of the traditional trade-offs long-held sacrosanct in the furniture industry. By leveraging the vertical linkages in its value system, IKEA's strategy is rare, in demand and difficult to imitate – it is well entrenched at the deep end of the industry profit pool.

Source: Adapted from Normann, R. and Ramirez, R.. 'From value chain to value constellation: designing interactive strategy', *Harvard Business Review*, 71(4), 1993, 65–77.

14

Win/loss analysis

Description and purpose

Win/loss analysis (WLA) is a cost-effective, insightful and ethical method for gathering and analysing information about your market, customers and competitors. WLA analysis identifies your customer's perceptions of specific sales situations and how you compared to your competitors. It provides a window as to why a customer is buying or not buying your products and/or services. Additionally, the analysis provides information about the performance of both your firm and your competitors. This information can then be actively used to focus sales staff more effectively in the marketplace and also to inform research and development of products.

WLA is a management tool that allows managers to understand the effectiveness of their sales team and the effectiveness of competitors. WLA requires the gathering of direct feedback from a client or potential client about why you won or lost a specific sale or contract. It must include both wins and losses. The wins tend to highlight your firm's strengths and your competition's weaknesses, while the losses highlight your firm's weaknesses and your competition's strengths.

The feedback provides information you can actively use to improve both the performance of your sales force and your existing products, and to guide your firm in the research and development of new products.

To be most effective, a win/loss programme needs to be established as an ongoing process conducted on a regular basis by a third-party supplier for maximum objectivity.

WLA is a unique tool that brings together all the elements of strategy – information about customers, competitors and your own firm – within the context of the most critical element for a business, the buying decision. As a market listening tool, it is designed to provide a firm with information that can actively be used to increase its sales. By seeking feedback directly from the target market and subjecting this to analysis, a firm can gain something of an objective understanding of its place in the market and use this to improve its position.

From win/loss interviews, a firm can identify how a competitor is developing its products and/or services or whether it has or has not delivered on promises. It can provide an avenue to reopen doors with former clients. As a tool, it makes existing and potential clients realise the commitment your firm has to maintaining good customer relationships.

The results of WLA provide information about sales performance, sales opportunities, market perception of yours and your competitors' products, and your competitors' strategies. It can provide a measurement of how your firm is positioned with decision makers and key influencers within a client's firm. When acted on, this information should enable your firm to improve sales, increase market share, understand the market to maximise business opportunities, and focus marketing and sales resources to increase revenue.

Strengths

WLA is a systematic analysis of nominated sales results – both wins and losses. It encompasses feedback from strategically important existing clients, former clients and potential clients. Regular and systematic WLA processes provides not only immediate feedback, but can also be used to compare and uncover trends over time.

There are numerous tactical and strategic benefits flowing from WLA. Tactical benefits tend to focus on sales performance, while strategic ones flow beyond the sales team to assist with product management, mergers and alliances, and product research and development. These are summarised in Table 14.1.

Table 14.1 Tactical and strategic benefits of WLA

Tactical benefits	*Strategic benefits*
■ Improve sales results by helping the sales team win more business	■ Increase firm profits and revenue over a longer period of time
■ Improve client retention by following up on sales wins to identify how/why you win business	■ Forecast revenue streams more accurately
■ Identify regularly why/how you lose against each of your competitors and devise ways to enhance your sales positioning	■ Enhance the product/service offering and mix
	■ Influence more timely product/service development
■ Establish an action plan to address gaps in perceptions that may exist between clients and the sales force	■ Alter the firm's culture to a more client service/needs focus
■ Change behaviour and culture to improve client service, maintenance programmes, or delivery based on accurate, timely feedback from clients	■ Select appropriate market alliances with increased confidence
	■ Support the firm's early warning system
■ Identify traits of your successful salespeople. Conversely, identify traits of unsuccessful salespeople	■ Identify competitor trends over time to enable action
■ Predict likelihood of winning/losing a sale more accurately and therefore identify when to walk away from business	
■ Change the sales mindset from one of making excuses for sales loss	

Source: Adapted from Naylor, E., 'Increasing sales through win/loss analysis', *Competitive Intelligence Magazine*, 5(5), 2002, 5–8.

The WLA process allows for direct feedback on what the decision-making criteria employed by your clients, in awarding your firm their business or taking it to a competitor, are. An expert interviewer can go beyond the standard questionnaire to probe a client and give him or her a chance to directly express their needs and preferences. This in turn gives your firm the opportunity to make meaningful changes acting on customer advice to improve practices and win new sales.

The benefits of conducting WLA extend beyond providing tactics to improve sales. WLA also has an impact on marketing, product improvement, and research and development. Information coming out of WLA can be distributed throughout the firm to assist in overall performance improvements. The results obtained from WLA may be used to inform other strategic programmes within a firm. For example, it may assist in the development of training programmes for sales staff or assist in product improvement projects.

The WLA process will give an indication in real time of the market's response to new business strategies and products. It will enable the firm to identify and respond to trends over time in the market and assist in sales forecasting. If undertaken in a systematic way, it will assist in growing revenues both in the short and long term.

In summary, WLA establishes a market listening and positioning tool with consistent analysis allowing for improved and informed decision making in an organisation by:

- helping decision makers understand the customer's perspective
- providing objective input into sales and marketing strategies
- identifying opportunities, including target markets, key sales propositions and winning attitudes
- improving business performance at the expense of competitors.

Weaknesses

WLA is based on data obtained from interviews arising out of sales results. It is to that extent reactive and event driven. Care must be taken to ensure that a good mix of sales results are followed up. Results will be skewed, for example if in one round of WLA, only successful sales to existing clients are analysed.

A key weakness of this process is that interviews are only as good as the interviewer conducting them. When an interviewer is inexperienced or has not been thoroughly briefed on the sensitivities of the market in question, the quality of the data obtained will be compromised. An inexperienced interviewer may lack the confidence to ask questions beyond those contained in the standard questionnaire developed for the WLA process. Even the most experienced interviewer will be unable to gain all the useful information potentially available if they are not sufficiently aware of the issues in the market to know when to probe for further detail in an interview and when it is not relevant.

There is no value in information gathered if it is not systematically disseminated to those who can act on it. As is a danger, in a firm, with any information-gathering process, it is possible for the results of WLA to end up being fiercely guarded rather than distributed. On the other hand, it is possible to undermine the process by giving all of the results to everyone and no one having time to read them, let alone act on them.

The value of WLA will only be as good as the system set up to educate interested parties of the results. Information taken out of context – for example, in an attempt to extrapolate widely from one individual analysis – will not be reliable. The true value of WLA is in the ongoing process.

WLA must be conducted systematically and in a timely fashion. Interviews must be organised and followed up as soon as possible after the sale is won or lost. Delay in interviewing may result in inaccurate recall, so the analysis performed does not reflect the real reasons behind the decision to do business with your firm or with your competition. WLA itself should be conducted regularly to give truly comparable results. The analysis must not, for example, be shelved while more important issues are dealt with, as sporadic WLA will not give reliable information.

It is important to note that the strategic implications of WLA are highly dependent on the quality of the raw data. The raw data gathered from clients should be free from any political or strategic bias and subjective perspective – particularly where employees within a firm may distort information. The fact that WLA focuses on sales results may lead to a politicising of the process within a firm. The sales team may be reluctant to cooperate fully with the process if they feel they are being singled out unfairly. Other parts of the firm may try to ambush the process to push their own agendas. The team responsible for running WLA must be very carefully chosen and trained to ensure the members fully understand the WLA process and are prepared to implement it properly.

How to do it

Numerous writers in the field suggest that there are up to seven steps to consider in creating and implementing a WLA process. These steps are shown in Figure 14.1.

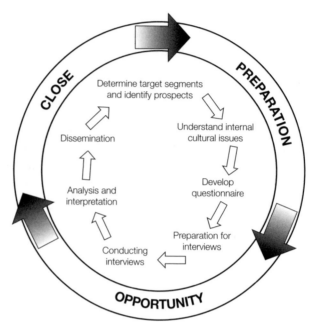

Figure 14.1 The win/loss process

Each of the steps in the WLA process are described below.

Step 1: Determine the target segments and identify prospects

Target the right accounts to analyse and the right interval to conduct analysis. A good starting point is to look at the accounts that generate most of your firm's revenue (the 80/20 rule – 80 per cent of a firm's revenue comes from 20 per cent of its customers). However, other considerations in choosing whom to interview may include whether your firm wishes to pick up business from particular potential clients or ex-clients, or whether there are plans to introduce new products to the market. Specific companies that meet the firm's chosen criteria need to be identified and singled out and reviewed to ensure that the targets are worth the investment.

Experts in this technique suggest that you need to start by segmenting the specific market group or target, particularly if the purpose of WLA is to identify sales sources. Once target segments and their criteria are identified, key information needs to be collected to quality potential prospects.

The interval over which you run your WLA will depend on your firm's requirements. Monthly analysis requires a greater commitment of time and money, but will provide very quick market feedback. Some firms prefer to run a large win/loss study annually. The interval chosen will also be affected by how quickly you wish to be able to act on the information you obtain.

Step 2: Understand internal cultural issues

Understanding the firm's culture will provide a guide as to how information will be used. For example, in a learning and consultative culture, sales representatives and their managers might become highly involved in both the collection and evaluation of information.

It is also important to ensure that involvement in the process extends beyond the sales team. Other key stakeholders need to be clearly identified, and creating cross-functional teams may be a way to addressing the differing needs of critical groups.

The results of WLA have implications that go beyond increasing sales. To get the most out of the process, the team running the programme should include members from other departments and have the support of senior management.

The objectives of the programme must also be well defined. The roles of designing and implementing the programme should be clearly understood, as these may be assigned to different people.

Those who are likely to be affected by the information obtained from the WLA programme should be educated about the process to ensure they support it. This should reduce internal resistance to WLA. Some staff, particularly in sales, may feel that their performance is being unfairly singled out for attention by the programme. Staff should be reassured that the WLA programme has wider implications for the firm than simply monitoring the performance of individual's in the sales team.

The decision must be made whether to use an independent third party to conduct the interviews or whether to use your sales team. Use of a third-party interviewer has cost implications. It will also require a commitment of time from internal staff to brief the interviewer. The use the firm intends to make of the information will also direct the decision of who conducts interviews. When the results of the interviews will be used in part to evaluate the performance of members of the sales team, it is suggested that sales involvement in the interview process be kept to a minimum. However, parallel interviews of client and sales representative can reveal valuable information about the different perceptions they have of the same sales negotiations.

Step 3: Develop the questionnaire

A WLA questionnaire needs to cover principally four key areas:

- *Sales attributes*. This will cover the professionalism of your sales team, the quality of the relationship your firm has with the client, and the esteem in which the client holds your firm compared to your competitors.

- *Company reputation*. This includes questions about the perception of your firm's and your competitors' image in the marketplace, the stability of your firm, and its reliability as a supplier and the quality and performance of your products.

- *Product attributes*. This is a wide area basically covering whether your products actually perform as promoted and covers issues of price and technology.

- *Service issues*. These questions will cover the delivery and implementation, maintenance and after-sales service, and training provided to clients.

Depending on the purpose of the WLA, other areas that might be included in the questionnaire could address matters relating to how the purchase decision will be made: will it be made by a group or individual? What are the decision criteria? When will the decision be made? Are there other stakeholders involved?

Another consideration will be the sophistication of the analysis you plan to carry out on the results. When analysis will stop at the quick identification of market trends, numerous detailed questions may not be necessary. When statistical analysis is the aim, the information must be sufficiently detailed to address the required level of analysis and still be of practical value.

Standard issues need to be identified in the questionnaire to ensure that the data from multiple interviews can be effectively analysed together and over time. At the same time, some flexibility in the interview process will enable valuable exploration of individual situations.

Step 4: Preparation for the interviews

The interviewer now needs to be briefed about the significance of winning or losing each sale. To get the most out the interview, the interviewer must be aware of all relevant details and sensitivities of the sale/non-sale being investigated.

When an interviewer does not fully understand the background of a particular sale negotiation, he or she is unlikely to be able to stray from the standard form questionnaire to probe for detailed situation-specific feedback. Specific and detailed information can greatly enhance the overall value of the WLA process.

Step 5: Conducting interviews

Carefully consider how you wish to go about conducting interviews. This decision will depend to an extent of whether you plan to use a third-party interviewer or your own sales team. Experts in this field highly recommend the use of an independent third party to avoid interview results being skewed by any pre-existing relationship between a salesperson and his or her client. For example, the interviewer may direct the responses they receive with unintentional body language cues.

One option is to conduct interviews by telephone. This is a common practice in the US and is quite time and cost effective. However, in some situations – for example, for big-ticket purchase items – it may be preferable to conduct face-to-face interviews in order to obtain optimal results in a particular situation. Here you will need to rely on your sales team to advise when face-to-face interviews would be better. It should be noted that face-to-face interviews provide a much great opportunity to garner in-depth information and to build on customer relationships than telephone interviews.

Interviews should be conducted as close in time to the actual sale/non-sale so to avoid memories of the negotiations fading. Some firms may also interview the salesperson involved in the particular sale/non-sale to investigate differences between the firm's own internal perception of the negotiations and those of the client.

Obtaining information that addresses specific issues ensures meaningful comparison can be made when analysing the responses obtained at individual interviews.

Step 6: Analysis and interpretation

Once the interviews are completed, the results need to be tallied and analysed. The interviewer will generally summarise each completed interview and provide an analysis of key trends or issues identified as a result of the interviews in a report. If the interviews are carried out by internal staff, then training and support must be provided to carry out these tasks effectively and to aid with the report development. WLA must be given clear priority over other duties when analysis is due to be done. The value of WLA is compromised by sporadic rather than regular analysis.

As the WLA programme continues over time, trends will emerge from the analytical results. These need to be interpreted in light of the firm's strategic and competitive intentions.

Furthermore, over time, WLA becomes more valuable in identifying trends that impact product development and sales forecasting. Companies have been known to adjust their product plans in light of client feedback from WLA.

Step 7: Dissemination

The report and results can now be disseminated. There will be information arising out of WLA that is relevant to different departments in the firm such as research and development, marketing and sales. The programme team should ensure that each department receives the information relevant to it. This should hopefully increase the likelihood that the information is read and supports decision making in the appropriate department. The results may be presented in different forms depending on preferences.

Different staff will have different preferences for how the WLA results should be communicated to them – from verbal presentations at the completion of interviews to half-yearly reports. For example, a WLA programme where senior management receive a monthly report summarising quantified results, while the sales team receive results incorporated into their regular e-mail alerts.

Properly conducted WLA is one of the most valuable tools for sales account strategies. WLA helps firms understand the value of customers and the cost of retaining them versus acquiring new ones. Simultaneously, it allows firms to capture best practices in sales and identify trends to enhance future revenue streams.

Microsoft Business Solutions

Microsoft Business Solutions (now known as Microsoft Dynamics) provides a line of financial, customer relationship and supply chain management solutions to help businesses improve their performance. Delivered through a network of specialised partners, these integrated business management solutions work with Microsoft software to streamline processes across an entire business and include applications and services for retailers, manufacturers, wholesale distributors and service companies, doing business domestically or in multiple countries.

At the time of this case study, Microsoft Business Solutions was well positioned to be the dominant player in the mid-level financial software market with its Great Plains solution. This solution provides a financial, analytics and business management system that unifies data and processes across a business, integrating easily with other solutions, and connecting employees, customers and suppliers regardless of time or location.

With a strong product and a large sales force, Microsoft had the potential of winning the majority of competitive opportunities.

The challenge facing Microsoft Business Solutions was to understand the competitive environment in order to leverage its strengths and capitalise on the weaknesses of its competitors with the goal of winning the lion's share of opportunities.

Understanding the environment

Primary Intelligence conducted a win/loss assessment of Microsoft Great Plains' previous 100 opportunities, comprised of 50 wins and 50 losses. Information was gathered on purchase selection criteria, primary competitors' strengths and weaknesses, the efficacy of various marketing activities and customer satisfaction.

Analysis of the gathered information yielded a clear picture of the competitive environment, focusing on areas of differentiation – both in product and in sales methodology. It became apparent that Microsoft Business Solutions had clear advantages in certain areas that had not been previously identified, and that, although the competition was strong in most areas, there were specific weaknesses that contributed to Microsoft wins.

Learning from their losses

Two important, related things Microsoft Business Solutions learned from their losses were that: (a) prospects didn't perceive that they or their partners understood their needs; and (b) one of the ways prospects expressed this was in lower marks for industry experience and knowledge.

Because of the knowledge gained in the win/loss report, Microsoft Business Solutions recently announced industry-focused strategies in four major industry sectors that they believe will help them and their partners be more successful in the mid-market.

Leveraging the data

As part of the Primary Intelligence solution, senior analysts helped Microsoft Business Solutions leverage the data in the report to improve their competitive position in the marketplace, provide even further insight into the competitive sales cycle that Microsoft Business Solutions' channel partners currently face in today's market conditions, and gain important insight into potential new strategies and programmes that could be implemented to ultimately help the partner win more business in competitive situations.

Keeping current

Another valuable tool for Microsoft Business Solutions was the comparison Primary Intelligence provided with the previous year's win/loss study. Analysis of ▶

the differences showed that certain shortcomings had been addressed, while new potential problems had surfaced. It also showed the progress, or lack of progress, of the competition, making it possible to assess new threats and exploit new opportunities.

This ongoing assessment made it possible for Microsoft Business Solutions to track the dynamics of the industry, respond quickly to change and stay one step ahead of the competition.

Source: Primary Intelligence, www.primary-intel.com/solutions/winloss.aspx (accessed 12 March 2006).

Index

ABA (activity-based accounting),
    176
ABM (activity-based
    management), 176
acceptance, lack of, for STEEP
    analysis, 154
accounting equation in FRSA, 67–
    8
accounting methods, effect on
    income statements, 71
accounting periods, defined, 68
accounts receivable ratios in FRSA,
    73–4
accounts receivable to sales ratio,
    74
accounts receivable turnover ratio,
    74
accuracy of collected data, 16
acid test ratio, 77
acquisitions, value chain analysis
    and, 175
activity-based accounting (ABA),
    176
activity-based management
    (ABM), 176
advocacy issues, 110
airline industry case study (Five
    Forces Industry Analysis), 97–
    9
alliances, value chain analysis
    and, 175
*Almanac of Business and Industrial
    Financial Ratios*, 84
ambiguity, 11
analysis
    challenges addressed by, 10–12
    cognitive biases in, 18–19
    competencies for conducting,
        19–20
    data collection, role in, 16–17
    defined, 6–7, 15–16
    as element of strategic thinking,
        19
    generic process to, 16
    purpose of, 6
    reasons for lack of, 13–14
    reasons for need for, 8–10
    results of, 6
    scientific method comparison,
        15
    warnings concerning, 17–18
analysis techniques. *See* BCG
    matrix; competitor analysis;
    driving forces analysis Five

Forces Industry Analysis;
    FRSA; issue analysis; product
    life cycle analysis; scenario
    analysis; STEEP analysis;
    SWOT analysis; value chain
    analysis; win/loss analysis
analytical dynamics, including in
    BCG matrix, 34–5
Andrews, Ken, 159
assessment in Five Forces Industry
    Analysis, 96–7
asset turnover ratios in FRSA, 74–5
assets, defined, 67
assumptions of competitors,
    identifying, 46–7, 52
attacking groups (issue response
    pattern), 113
attention groups (issue expansion
    map), 108
attentive public (issue expansion
    map), 108
average collection periods, 73–4
average inventory investment
    period, 72–3

balance sheets, defined, 68
bargaining (issue response
    pattern), 114
bargaining power
    of buyers, 91–2
    of suppliers, 91
BCG matrix
    case study, 36–7
    experience curve theory and, 24
    product life cycle and, 25
    purpose of, 23–4
    quadrants in, 25–6, 28
    steps in, 31–6
    strengths of, 28–9
    weaknesses of, 29–30
biases in analysis, 18–19
blurring (issue response pattern),
    113
Boston Consulting Group. *See*
    BCG matrix
brands (STEEP analysis case
    study), 157–8
broadband cable TV industry case
    study (BCG matrix), 36–7
Bureau van Dijk Electronic
    Publishing, 84
business management
    defined, 3
    requirements of, 15

business units. *See* SBUs (strategic
    business units)
buyers, bargaining power of, 91–2

Cannondale Bicycle Corporation
    case study (SWOT analysis),
    169–70
capabilities of competitors,
    determining, 46, 52
capital market analysis ratios in
    FRSA, 79–82
capitulation (issue response
    pattern), 114
case studies
    BCG matrix, 36–7
    competitor analysis, 50–2
    driving forces analysis, 63–6
    Five Forces Industry Analysis,
        97–100
    FRSA, 87–8
    issue analysis, 115–16
    product life cycle analysis, 132–
        3
    scenario analysis, 144–7
    STEEP analysis, 157–8
    SWOT analysis, 169–70
    value chain analysis, 186–7
    win/loss analysis, 198–200
'cash cows' (in BCG matrix), 26–7
cash flow, 70
cessation (issue response pattern),
    114
cognitive biases in analysis, 18–19
collecting data. *See* data collection
commitment, escalating, 18
comparison grids, 48
comparison of ratios in FRSA, 82
    industrial comparisons, 82–5
    performance history
        comparisons, 85–6
competencies
    for conducting analysis, 19–20
    defined, 3, 9
competition, intensity of, 92–3
competitive advantage, defined,
    3–4
Competitive Advantage (Porter), 171
competitive position (in BCG
    matrix), 25
competitor analysis, 36, 174
    with BCG matrix, 28–9
    case study, 50–2
    purpose of, 39–40
    steps in, 42–50

strengths of, 41
weaknesses of, 41
competitor comparisons in ratio
  analysis, 69
competitor matrices, constructing
  for BCG matrix, 33
complexity, increasing, 9
computer-generated econometric
  model (scenario analysis),
  136
consistency in scenario analysis,
  142
consolidated financial statements,
  segmented financial
  statements versus, 86
content analysis, 104
control, illusion of, 18
Corporate Information, 83
cross-impact method (scenario
  analysis), 137
cultural issues, internal, 195–6
current assets, defined, 67
current issues, 109
current liabilities, defined, 68
current ratio, 76–7
current strategy of competitors,
  46, 51
customer value analysis, 174

D&B–Duns Financial Records
  Plus® (DFR), 83
data collection
  in Five Forces Industry Analysis,
  94–6
  role in analysis, 16–17
Dean, Joel, 117
debt to assets ratio, 75
debt to equity ratio, 75
decision scenarios in scenario
  analysis, 142
deductive reduction, 137
Dell case study (FRSA), 87–8
Delphi method (scenario
  analysis), 136–7
Delphi panels, 104–5
defusing issues (issue response
  pattern), 113
DFA. See driving forces analysis
digital music industry case study
  (driving forces analysis), 63–6
diversification scenarios, 138
diversified businesses, effect on
  STEEP analysis, 154
'dogs' (in BCG matrix),
  27
driving forces analysis
  case study, 63–6
  purpose of, 53–4
  steps in, 56–63
  strengths of, 54–5
  weaknesses of, 55
Dupont case study (product life
  cycle analysis), 132

earnings per share (EPS), 80
emerging issues, 108–9
entry barriers, role of, 90
environment, levels of, 149–50
environmental analysis. See STEEP
  analysis

environmental boundaries,
  establishing (STEEP analysis),
  154
EPS (earnings per share), 80
escalating commitment, 18
evaluation in Five Forces Industry
  Analysis, 96–7
events in STEEP analysis, defined,
  155
experience curve theory, BCG
  matrix and, 24
external environment, SWOT
  analysis, 159–60, 162–3
external opportunities
  internal weaknesses relative to,
  167
  matching with internal
  strengths, 167
external threats
  internal weaknesses relative to,
  168
  matching with internal
  strengths, 167–8

false alarm scenario (scenario
  analysis case study), 145
financial ratio and statement
  analysis. See FRSA
financial statement analysis,
  defined, 67. See also FRSA
financial statements
  components of, 68–9
  consolidated versus segmented
  financial statements, 85–6
Financial Times, 83
Five Forces Industry Analysis
  buyers, bargaining power of,
  91–2
  case studies, 97–100
  competition, intensity of, 92–3
  entry barriers, role of, 90
  market displacement, threat of,
  92
  objective of, 89–90
  steps in, 94–7
  strengths of, 93
  suppliers, bargaining power of,
  91
  weaknesses of, 94
fixed assets, defined, 67
fixed charge coverage, 76
forces, defined, 53
forecasting
  future direction of issues in
  STEEP analysis, 156–7
  in issue analysis, 104–5
  formation stage (issue life
  cycle), 105–6
  formatting competitive analysis
  results, 47
fractionation of trends, 155
FRSA (financial ratio and
  statement analysis), 67
  accounting equation in, 67–8
  accounts receivable ratios in,
  73–4
  asset turnover ratios in, 74–5
  capital market analysis ratios in,
  79–82
  case study, 87–8

financial ratios, list of, 80–2
financial statements,
  components of, 68–9
  inventory ratios in, 73
  liquidity analysis ratios in, 76–7
  profitability analysis ratios in,
  78–9
  ratio comparison in, 82, 85–6
  ratios, assessing appropriateness
  of, 69
  shareholder returns analysis
  ratios in, 79–82
  solvency analysis ratios in, 75–6
  steps in, 72
  strengths of, 69–70
  weaknesses of, 70–2
future goals of competitors, 46,
  50–1
future uncertainty, dealing with,
  143–4

GE (General Electric), 23
general environment in STEEP
  analysis, 149–50
general public (issue expansion
  map), 108
globalisation, 8, 56
Google Finance, 83
government regulation scenario
  (scenario analysis case study),
  146
gross profit margin, 78–9
'groupthink', 18
growth rate
  plotting on BCG matrix, 32
  of SBUs/SBLs, measuring, 31
Growth/share portfolio matrix. See
  BCG matrix

identification groups (issue
  expansion map), 108
IKEA case study (value chain
  analysis), 186–7
illusion of control, 18
imitators, abundance of, 9
impact/probability matrix in
  scenario analysis case study,
  144–7
impacts of trends, 155–6
implications of STEEP analysis,
  157
inaccuracy in STEEP analysis, 153
income statements, defined, 68
inductive reduction, 137
industrial comparisons in FRSA,
  82–5
industry analysis. See Five Forces
  Industry Analysis
industry norms, reliance on, 70–1
industry profit pool, mapping in
  value chain analysis, 182–4
industry scenarios, 138
industry-wide comparisons in
  ratio analysis, 69
information, knowledge versus, 8–
  9
information collection in Five
  Forces Industry Analysis, 94–
  6
information retrieval, 12

institutionalised issues, 109
intangible assets, 70
integration, value chain analysis and, 174–5
interest coverage, 76
interest groups, 106
internal cost analysis in value chain analysis, 181–2
internal differentiation analysis in value chain analysis, 182
internal environment, SWOT analysis, 159, 162–3
internal strengths, matching with external opportunities/ threats, 167–8
internal weaknesses, relative to external opportunities/ threats, 167, 168
interpretation
    in STEEP analysis, 153
    in win/loss analysis, 197–8
interviews in win/loss analysis, 196–7
intuitive method (scenario analysis), 136
inventory ratios in FRSA, 73
inventory to sales ratio, 73
issue analysis
    case studies, 115–16
    purpose of, 101–2
    steps in, 104–15
    strengths of, 103
    weaknesses of, 103–4
issue assessment in issue analysis, 109–11
issue expansion map, 108
issue identification in issue analysis, 104–9
issue impact (assessing issues), 109–10
issue life cycle
    four-stage progression, 105–6
    seven-stage progression, 106–8
issue timing, 108–9
issues (STEEP analysis)
    forecasting future direction of, 156–7
    relating trends to, 156
issues distance (assessing issues), 109

joint ventures, value chain analysis and, 175

Kellogg's case study (product life cycle analysis), 132–3
Key Business Ratios on the Web, 83
knowledge, information versus, 8–9
knowledge economy, 9

latent issues, 108
learning function (in experience curve), 24
learning scenarios in scenario analysis, 142
legislative formalisation stage (issue life cycle), 106

leverage analysis ratios. See solvency analysis ratios in FRSA
LexisNexis, 83
liabilities, defined, 68
liquidity analysis ratios in FRSA, 76–7
long-term liabilities, defined, 68

macroenvironmental analysis. See STEEP analysis
magnitude of trends, 155
management choices, effect on financial statements, 71
mapping industry profit pool in value chain analysis, 182–4
market attractiveness (in BCG matrix), 25
market displacement, threat of, 92
market growth rate. See growth rate
market modification (product life cycle analysis), 122
marketing mix modification (product life cycle analysis), 122
mergers, value chain analysis and, 175
Microsoft Business Solutions case study (win/loss analysis), 198–200
Minnegasco case study (issue analysis), 115
misperceptions of STEEP analysis, 154
mixed scenario method (scenario analysis), 137

negative impacts of trends, 155–6
net profit margin, 79
neutral impacts of trends, 156
noncurrent assets, defined, 67

OneSource, 84
operational decisions, defined, 5
opportunities
    defined, 165
    listing in SWOT analysis, 165
    ranking in SWOT analysis, 166
    strategy development in SWOT analysis, 166–9
organisational structure, value chain analysis and, 175
overconfidence, 18
oversimplification, 19
owners' equity, defined, 68

P/E (price/earnings) ratio, 80
penetration (product life cycle analysis), 120, 129–30
performance history
    comparisons in FRSA, 85–6
    in ratio analysis, 69
    reliance on, 71
PEST analysis. See STEEP analysis
pharmaceutical industry case study
    Five Forces Industry Analysis, 99–100
    scenario analysis, 144–7

plausibility in scenario analysis, 142
PLC. See product life cycle analysis
PLC, BCG matrix and, 25
plotting SBUs/SBLs on BCG matrix, 32–3
politicisation stage (issue life cycle), 106
Porter, Michael, 39, 89, 171–5, 178
portfolio matrix. See BCG matrix
position statements, defined, 68
positive impacts of trends, 156
PP (public policy). See issue analysis
price/earnings ratio, 80
'Pricing policies for new products' (Dean), 117
primary activities in value chain analysis, 172, 178–80
prior hypothesis bias, 19
prioritising issues, 110–11
'problem children' (in BCG matrix), 27
product life cycle, BCG matrix and, 25
product life cycle analysis
    case studies, 132–3
    purpose of, 117–25
    steps in, 128–32
    strengths of, 126
    weaknesses of, 126–8
product modification (product life cycle analysis), 122
profitability analysis ratios in FRSA, 78–9
public environmental intelligence, 101
public issue scenarios, 138
public policy. See issue analysis

qualitative methods of scenario analysis, 136–8
quantitative methods of scenario analysis, 136
quantitative models in scenario analysis, 142
questionnaires in win/loss analysis, 196
quick ratio, 77

radar charts, 47–8
ranking
    in driving forces analysis, 60–1
    SWOT analysis factors, 166
rate of change for trends, 155
ratio analysis, defined, 67. See also FRSA
ratio comparison in FRSA, 82
    industrial comparisons, 82–5
    performance history comparisons, 85–6
ratios, assessing appropriateness of, 69
regulation/litigation stage (issue life cycle), 106
relative market share
    plotting on BCG matrix, 32
    of SBUs/SBLs, measuring, 31–2
reliability of collected data, 16

representativeness bias, 19
research needs, identifying in
　scenario analysis, 142
resistance (issue response pattern),
　114
response patterns in issue
　analysis, 111–15
Rhodes-Blakeman Associates
　(RBA), 85
ROA (return on assets) ratio, 78
ROE (return on equity) ratio, 78

SBLs (strategic business lines)
　assigning strategies to, 34
　measuring growth rate of, 31
　measuring relative market share
　　of, 31–2
　plotting on BCG matrix, 32–3
　segmentation of, 31
SBUs (strategic business units)
　assigning strategies to, 34
　defining in value chain
　　analysis, 178
　measuring growth rate of, 31
　measuring relative market share
　　of, 31–2
　plotting on BCG matrix, 32–3
　segmentation of, 31
scale function (in experience
　curve), 24
scenario analysis
　case study, 144–7
　purpose of, 135–6
　qualitative methods, 136–8
　quantitative methods, 136
　scenario types in, 137–8
　steps in, 140–4
　strengths of, 139
　success factors in, 138
　weaknesses of, 140
scenario development, 104
scenarios
　defined, 135
　types of, 137–8
scientific method, analysis
　comparison, 15
SCIP (Society of Competitive
　Intelligence Professionals), 19
scope of scenario analysis, 141
segmented financial statements,
　consolidated financial
　statements versus, 86
selective issues, 110
self-regulation scenario (scenario
　analysis case study), 145–6
semi-log graphs, 32
sensitivity scenarios, 138
share momentum graph, 35
shareholder returns analysis ratios
　in FRSA, 79–82
short-term orientation, STEEP
　analysis versus, 153–4
simplification of problems, 19
situation analysis. See SWOT
　analysis
skimming (product life cycle
　analysis), 120, 129
Skyminder, 84
societal issues, 109
Society of Competitive

Intelligence Professionals
　(SCIP), 19
solvency analysis ratios in FRSA,
　75–6
specialisation function (in
　experience curve), 24
speed of change, 9
stakeholders, identifying for
　scenario analysis, 141
Standard & Poor's Industry
　Surveys, 84
'stars' (in BCG matrix), 26
statement of changes in owner's
　equity, defined, 68
STEEP analysis
　case study, 157–8
　environmental levels in, 149–50
　purpose of, 149–52
　STEEP scenarios versus, 137–8
　steps in, 155–7
　strengths of, 152–3
　variables in, 150–2
　weaknesses of, 153–4
STEEP scenarios, STEEP analysis
　versus, 137–8
strategic business lines. See SBLs
strategic business units. See SBUs
strategic cost management, 174
strategic decisions, defined, 5
strategic evaluation, 36
strategic issues, defined, 162
strategic management, defined, 3
strategic outsourcing, 175
strategic planning, defined, 4
strategic thinking, analysis in, 19
strategy development
　in Five Forces Industry Analysis,
　　97
　management decisions in, 4–5
　in SWOT analysis, 166–9
strengths
　defined, 165
　listing in SWOT analysis, 165
　ranking in SWOT analysis, 166
　strategy development in SWOT
　　analysis, 166–8
suppliers, bargaining power of, 91
supply chain management, 175
support activities in value chain
　analysis, 172, 180–1
survey techniques, 104–5
sustainable growth rate analysis,
　35
SWOT analysis
　case study, 169–70
　purpose of, 159–63
　steps in, 165–9
　strengths of, 163
　weaknesses of, 164

tactical decisions, defined, 5
technical issues, 110
termination (issue response
　pattern), 114
Thomson Reuters, 83
threats
　defined, 165
　listing in SWOT analysis, 165
　ranking in SWOT analysis, 166
　strategy development in SWOT

analysis, 167–8
time, lack of, 11
times interest earned ratio, 76
timing (of issues), 108–9
total disclosure scenario (scenario
　analysis case study), 146
trend analysis with BCG matrix,
　28
trends
　in driving forces analysis, 53–4,
　　57
　identifying for scenario
　　analysis, 141
　in STEEP analysis,
　　155–6

UK Companies Office, 83
uncertainties
　identifying for scenario
　　analysis, 141–2
　in STEEP analysis, 153
undermining groups (issue
　response pattern), 113
universal issues, 110

value chain analysis
　case study, 186–7
　primary activities in, 172, 178–
　　80
　purpose of, 171–5
　steps in, 178–85
　strengths of, 175–6
　subsets of, 174–5
　support activities in, 172, 180–1
　value chain links,
　　174
　weaknesses of, 176–7
value-creating activities,
　identifying in value chain
　analysis, 178–81
Value Line Investment Survey,
　84
variables in STEEP analysis,
　150–2
VCA. See value chain analysis
vertical linkage analysis in value
　chain analysis, 184–5
visual competitor strength grids,
　47–9

weaknesses
　defined, 165
　listing in SWOT analysis, 165
　ranking in SWOT analysis, 166
　strategy development in SWOT
　　analysis, 167, 168–9
win/loss analysis
　case study, 198–200
　purpose of, 189–90
　steps in, 194–8
　strengths of, 190–2
　weaknesses of, 192–3
WLA. See win/loss analysis
working capital, 77
Worldscope Fundamentals, 84

Xerox case study (issue analysis),
　115–16

Yahoo! Finance UK, 82